Society Today

Society Today:
Compiled Essays in Contemporary Anthropological Research

Edited by

Mr. Milonjyoti Borgohain
Dr. Dhritiman Sharma

KALPAZ

ISBN 9789353242435

First Published, 2020

Published by

Kalpaz Publications
C-30, Satyawati Nagar,
Delhi – 110052
Ph.: 011-47034999, 9811692060
www.kalpazpublications.com
E-mail: kalpaz@hotmail.com

Printed at: G. Print Process, Delhi

Contents

Foreword

It gives me immense pleasure to know that the book, "Society Today: Compiled Essays in Contemporary Anthropological Research" is going to publish as such kind of books are necessary to highlight the expanding scope of anthropological understanding pertaining to present-day social issues.

I am glad to learn that Mr. Milonjyoti Borgohain and Dr. Dhritiman Sharma has made an incessant effort to compile research articles addressing multiples cases and issues of the rural societies from across the country. Therefore, I welcome such a noble venture and I hope other engaged in the field of empirical research would follow this example and engage themselves in producing literature of this type, which would help not only to enrich their knowledge and experience but will add to the literature on rural Indian culture published so far.

I wish both of them success and luck.

Upala Barua

Signature

(UPALA BARUA)

Head, Department of Anthropology

Cotton University, Guwahati, Assam

Preface

This book is a compilation of empirical research works from different fields of anthropology. It explores the recent trends in emic approaches to address multiple issues confronting the changing rural societies. The first article on the topic of beads, entitled *Folklore and social science with special reference to Adi beads*. This topic of beads has been studied in archeology, anthropology, history from various perspectives, but Mr Perme has done an extensive research on the basis of the folklores related to the beads. Through the analysis of the folklores, he has gone to the depth of the beads and how these beads are very important in Adi and all Tanii groups societies is also shown. This article is useful for the researchers in history, folklore, anthropology and archeology and also economics, to understand various perspectives of tribal and culture through beads.

The second article entitled Syncretism in *Social Science with special reference to the Noctes of Arunachal*, by Chandan Kumar Boruah is an extensive work on the Nocte community in the topic of syncretism. Syncretism means combination of two contradictory beliefs in socio-cultural, religious and political life. Mr Boruah has done very extensive research and has gone to the areas of eastern Arunachal and has collected a large amount of data, many of which are collected for the first time. He has contributed a video among the Noctes in youtube as well.

The third article by Dhritiman Sharma entitled *Changing aspects of fieldwork traditions in Anthropology*, is on the history and development of fieldwork traditions in anthropology from Franz Boas till present. The article stresses on the reducing time framework of fieldwork with proper justifications at present, as change is found in every dimensions, and without change, a trend may be extinct.

The fourth article is by E Tamil Selvan, entitled *Tribal development and the Irulas*. With this article, we are heading towards Southern Anthropology of India. So far, we are mostly connected with the universities of the North, East and North East, but with the help of E Tamil Selvan, we are collaborating with South Indian Anthropology. The article speaks about the tribal development policies in the south and how the Irulas are getting affected from positive and negative dimensions of culture.

The fifth article entitled *Exploring Cultural Ecology in North East India: A Study among the Tai Khamti of Arunachal Pradesh* by Heerock Jyoti Baruah illustrates the importance of natural resource towards the development of indigenous cultural traits. This study addresses the socio-economic constraits evolving from non compliant resource management policies.

The sixth article entitled *Current Social Changing Scenario in Musahar Scheduled Caste of Bih*ar by Jokhan Sharma discusses the changing scenario of scheduled caste communities concentrating on the "Musahar" of Bihar.

The seventh article entitled *An ethnography of food among the Khasis of Wahmaw-Lyngdiar locality of Mawsynram village, East Khasi hills district, Meghalaya* by Leena Laskar observes the traditional diatery habits of the Khasis.

The eighth article entitled *Socio-demographic determinants and their effects on Infant mortality among two tribal population groups of Dhemaji districts, Assam, Northeast India* by Milonjyoti Borgohain is about infant mortality among the tribal people of Dhemaji, which is a burning issue in the interiors of North East India, as for proper health care facilities, one needs to run to Guwahati for a simple treatment too.

The ninth article entitled *A study on unpropitious women entrepreneurship in japi making activity: a case study of Nalbari district, Assam,* Nibedita Chaudhury highlights encouragement of women entrepreneurship plays an important role in improving the economic condition of a country.

The tenth article entitled *'A Study of Ethnomedicinal Plants used by Khamti Tribe of Narayanpur Block, Lakhimpur District'* by Nitusnata Saikia is on the traditional ethnomedicines of the Khampti tribe. Being a Botanist, Ms Saikia has highlighted well the importance of ethnomedicine and as they are knowledgeable about the plants, their contribution to anthropology makes very important aspect, especially in the field of medical anthropology.

The eleventh article entitled *The Kingdom of the Valiant and the Scrupulous: Details of the political settings of the Rajputs in Delwara and Goagaon, Sirohi District, Rajasthan* by Nyato Doji is on the Inter-village/ intra-village handling of affairs of the Rajputs, and other castes and sections of Delwara and Goagaon village. The study also focuses on the Marriage and land regulation; women, caste and kul vis-à-vis law converging on the Customary law, religious law, state law and local self-government persisting among the people of Delwara and Goagaon.

The twelfth article entitled *Mother's role in child socialization* by Promanita Bora is a very important article for the researchers, as well as for the new mothers of the society. Today, socialization process not that much strong as it was in the past, but has gone through a change. She has done an extensive bio-social research on this issue among the Mishings and in fact, the work is a holistic approach of the role of the mother in child socialization. Such articles are helpful for the society too, at present, along with academics.

The thirteenth article entitled *The Ethnomedicinal practices among the Mishings Tribe of Lakhimpur District, Assam* by Purabi Gogoi is a work done among the Mishings, on the topic of ethnomedicine. The study analyses how Mishing tribal people have their own way of diagnosis and therapy related to traditional medicine to cure different diseases.

The last article entitled *Megalith as living tradition in Arunachal Pradesh* by Shyamalee Gogoi is first hand research work on megaliths. In fact, megalith was discovered in Arunachal in 2010 by Directorate of Research, led by Tage Tada, JC Dutta and Nabajit Deuri, and based on that report; Shyamalee Gogoi becomes the first research scholar to work on the megalithic traditions in Arunachal Pradesh. She has covered the areas from West Kameng district to Eastern Arunachal, which is an extensive research work based on primary data collection. This article will be helpful for the researchers and students of history, anthropology and archeology.

Acknowledgement

Production of this anthropological research book was made possible by the contribution of quality time, ideas, designs, and intellectual creativities of many, students, colleagues, friends and well-wishers. We will be failing in our duty if we do not acknowledge the help and advice from them.

We place on record our appreciation and gratefulness to the contributors for this unique initiative and for the continuous support.

The authors of the units made their best attempt to provide the material according to our requirements in a short time and obliging to our request to take this work on priority basis. They showed the patience to review more than two or three times. We are deeply indebted to each one of them.

Milonjyoti Borgohain **Dhritiman Sharma**

List of Tables

List of Figures

List of the Contributors

Antony Perme is a Ph.D research scholar in the Department of Anthropology, Rajiv Gandhi University, Arunachal Pradesh.

Chandan Kumar Boruah is a Ph.D research scholar in the Department of Anthropology, Rajiv Gandhi University, Arunachal Pradesh.

Dhritiman Sharma is an assistant professor of anthropology in the Department of Anthropology, Rajiv Gandhi University, Arunachal Pradesh.

E Tamil Selvan is a Ph.D research scholar in the Department of Anthropology, University of Madras.

Heerock Jyoti Baruah is a Ph.D research scholar in the Department of Anthropology, University of Hyderabad, Telangana.

Jokhan Sharma is a Ph.D research scholar in the Department of Anthropology, Central University of Orissa, Koraput.

Leena Laskar has completed her Post-graduation in Anthrpology from Cotton University, Assam.

Milonjyoti Borgohain is an assistant professor of Anthropology at Moridhal College, Assam.

Nibedita Choudhury has completed her M.Phil from the Department of Anthropology, University of Hyderabad, Telangana.

Nitusnata Saikia is pursuing her B.Ed at Rajiv Gandhi University, Arunachal Pradesh.

Niyato Doji is a Ph.D research scholar in the Department of Anthropology, Rajiv Gandhi University, Arunachal Pradesh.

Dr. Promanita Bora is an Assistant Professor of Anthropology at Dibru College, Dibrugarh, Assam.

Purabi Gogoi is an M.Phil Research scholar at Assam University.

Shyamalee Gogoi is a Ph.D research scholar in the Department of Anthropolgy, Rajib Gandhi University, Arunachal Pradesh.

Chapter - 1

Folklore and social science with special reference to Adi Beads

Antoni Perme

Adi people are rich in oral literature. In absence of written records, they depict their past history through tales, legend and story-telling that passed down by older generations. Hence it is not possible to trace where, when and by what bead was made. As per Adi narration, it was Misummyang born of Pedong Nane who made the beads even before the existence of Tani (human). In fact, based on the research on the beads from ethno historical and anthropological perspectives, it has been seen that beads are currently holding an important place in folklore, through which we can trace the origin of the beads culture in human civilization, with special reference to the Adi people. This paper makes a modest attempt to find out the relation between the folklores and the beads and to analyze the meaning in relation to the beads, which may lead to an ethno historical approach to find out the beads in the society of the Adis.

Legend on Origin of Beads

Sedi Melo, the goddess or the creator of the universe was covered with dirt. Sedi Melo collected all the dirt and created the sky and the land out of it. Thus, the sky and the earth came into existence. Plain land, hills, vegetation, spring, streams, etc and later on Sedi Melo designed two suns (Mibang & Abrahan: 2002:15-16).

Sedi Melo/ Sedi gave birth to Dilling and Dilling gave birth to two children called Litung (male) and Limang (female), they grew up as a brother and sister and became adults. In course of time Limang became pregnant and gave birth to Tuye, Yepe and Pedong.

Genealogy as Follows

Sedi, Dilling, Litung, Tuye, Yepe, Pedong. Later Pedong Nane gave births to many children; (genealogy not in order) Doni, Domi, Dobi, Sili Sidong, Banji Banmang, Takom Tarii and many others and lastly gave birth to Robo (the spirit of jungle) and Nibo (the first human). The son of Pedong, Doni gave birth to Ninur (Ninurlomang) and Domi gave birth to Misum (Misummyiang). The son of Pedong, Dobi gave birth to Bisii (Bisiiyada). So it goes like- Pedong- Doni- Ninurlomang and Pedong- Domi- Misummyiang, and Pedong-Dobi- Bisiiyada.

Ninurlomang was great metal worker and owner of Arem like- Dangking, Barbang, Leeku-Lenong (metal plates, metallic utensils, pots etc). Bisiiyada was also a blacksmith and owner of Yoksa, Eyok, Egiing (sword, daw and axe etc).

Misum or Misummyiang as A Mother of Beads1

Like Ninurlomang and Bisiiyada, Misummyiang who was the sister of both had contributed in the existence of beads. She was the mother of beads, all the beads possessed by the Adi society in Arunachal Pradesh and some areas of Assam by Mishing tribes are believed to be made by Misummyiang she was the owner of valuable beads.

Aabang says:

"Keyum pedonge nane ke, ajii dirie diname,keyum misum e mone koh,kero miyang e moyong koh, keyum misum e yokmo kela, kero miyang e rempi ke, tadok beli e piname,tadok belo e yatname, misum sumko e kuro koh miyang aangko e kuli koh"

Or

"Keyum pedonge nane ke aji mambi duyi name, Pedong domi misum mone ko, Misum mone me pedong nane,gomung dodung e lurung kane,noh misum yokmoem molangka,miyang rempi em pilangka,keyum pedonge nane gumii dodungem luru rodem, keyum misum e mone kuro belo em yatlen tho kuli beli em pilen tho.

Meaning thereby:

"Misummyang was born of Pedong Nane whom the goddess instructs and bestowed the capability of making beads and she worked out, hence place where Misum lived we found the beads Kuro and Kuli.

So Misummyiang made the beads herself by clay and stones. In olden days there were soft rocks that could be even eaten up by the man. After finishing the shape and the size of beads she dried it on the sun light and took it to a river called doggo or Laying Asi where she drowned the beads for tempering. Since then bead has become hard and acquired the green and blue watery color.

Aabang says:

"keyum misume mone ke,doggo asii tesige, tadok beloem yatlen Tula misum yoggo laying asii tesig, keyum misume yokmo de yoggo parkingem rokyon Tula,doggo pargoem rokyon Tula,tadok beli e pinam dem tadok buying em buji likto,doggo langore asii langore tetor gela tadok langor e tetor gekai, doggo laying e asii laying e sising gelaa tadok laying e sising gekai,tadok buying em boji likto, tadok tolko e tolki lenkai"

Meaning thereby:

"Misum the expert carry out the task and made the bead and prepared the place at the laying Asi where she drowned and tempered the beads, as such the beads acquired the nature of its hardness and watery blue color".

Legend behind the possession of beads by Tani (human)

Archery competition[2]

Pedong Nane, the mother of millions gave birth to Robo and Nibo as her youngest child. Robo also called as Epom (spirit of jungle) and Nibo the Tani (human). Genealogically, Robo was elder to Nibo. Both of them were treated equally and respected in the society. The elder brother Robo has been described physically stronger and less intelligent in traditional myth and Nibo as physically weaker but more intelligent.

Since Robo and Nibo married and started living separately, the question of property division aroused. In the mean time, the owner of valuable Tadok, Misummyiang died, the society convinced Nibo to do burial of the death and he followed. As per the tradition Nibo has to take the possession of all beads. Robo protested and insisted that the property should be shared among the two brothers. An archery competition was arranged, on the condition that whoever could hit and stick his arrow on the target would get the property. A metal plate was placed at a distance as the target. Nibo was advised secretly to smear wax of the bee on the arrow. Robo was asked to shoot first. His arrow struck the target and broke the target partially instead of sticking on it. Next was Nibo's turn. He slowly released his arrow and hit the target, which stuck on it. Nibo won the competition and became the owner of the property of Misummyang (Mibang & Abrahan: 2002:57).

Competition for possession of beads[3]

There had been a competition between Nibo and Robo in many fields like – archery, fishing, trapping etc.

Aabang says:

"Misum mone ke kuro beloem kuli beliem yatlen rodem, Keyum pedong nane aji mambi ko duyi kaku ne,Pedong doro robo kolang pedong doni ko aji mambi duyi toku, pedong doro robo mela pedong doni aji dem keyum pedonge nane gumu dodunge lurung kakune, misum bangenge lirengte misum diyinge birsing, miyang derange birtang ko, misum sumkue kuro ko misum keldenge miyang keldenge keldak, pedong doro robo nolang pedong doni aji no, misum redengem biying redengem kuro redengem toki suto ka, pedong doro robo biying birtang redengem tua to, pedong doni aji misum sumku kuli kuro aro dem tua toh".

Or

Misum libu buru telo, tadok kelmang em keldung em, Biying kelmang em birtang kelmang em keldung em, Pedo doro robo biying birtang lirung em yua tho,Pedo doni aji tadok lirung em gakrek tho.

Meaning there by:

"As Misummyang made the beads, Pedong Nane later gave birth to Robo and Nibo. Of the two sons, Nibo was younger. Pedong Nane informed them of treasure that kept in cave and competition was arranged between the two brothers to have the treasures. The condition was that whoever discovered the hole of treasure would get the beads. Consequently, Robo by mistake hold the Biying Birtang(small green snake) and Nibo fortunately got the beads that kept in. As such Nibo won the competition and became the owner of valuable beads".

Legend Behind Why Evil Spirits Fear Beads and Amulets

Misummyang was the great smith of beads and bangles and Ninurlomang, the smith of tools and weapons. Once, the two smiths had a dispute with Banji-Banmang-the spirit who torments and inflicts diseases to humans.

Having been driven to the wall by the deadly and mischievous Banji-Banmang and his cohorts, Misummyang and Ninurlomang in the name of the Almighty Donyi-Polo taught these cunning spirits a lesson for their mischief and lies! Let Banji-Banmang sene! Their scandalous female chief tormented by the powerful beads! Let Banji jiri mone, the disgraceful one be frightened by my strong bangles and sonorous and healing going! Let them fear those so that men can live in peace.

Ninurlomang also prayed, "Oh Donyi Polo let my swords and the Emul, the metal necklaces frighten away all members of the cunning tribe for good! From today, let these valuable beads tools and weapon terrify all Banji-Banmang so that they desist from attacking men at will.

Donyi-Polo listened to their prayer with sympathy, then, he blessed all the amulets: beads, tools, bangles and swords with healing power. He also advised Misummyang and Ninurlomang to put the amulets on the body of sick to drive away the evil spirits.

Since then, Banji-Banmang and other evil spirit began to fear those amulets put on the body of human (Tayeng 2003:37-38).

Notes

1. This information was given by Bangkak pertin of parbuk , Ngik Perme of Bolung, Kolsul Apum (preist) and
2. The story was revealed by Okur Pertin of Bolung and Katu Lego of Dambuk.
3. This story narrated by Ammon Pertin, Osup Dai of bolung and Kolsul Apum of Dambuk.

References

Blackburn, Stuart, 2004, Memories of migration, European bulletin of Himalayan Research

Daniella, E. and P. Naomi, 2008, Green stone beads at the down of agriculture, National academy of science. 2008

Elwin, Varrier, 1957, A philosophy for NEFA, Directorate of Research, Govt. of Arunachal Pradesh, Itanagar

Lego, K, 2004, The exchange and distribution system in Adi, in Mibang and Behera (eds) Tribal villages in Arunachal Pradesh, Abhijeet Publication, Delhi

Mibang, T. and PT Abraham, 2002, Indian folk tales of North-East, Farsight Publishers, Delhi, 2002.

Nath, J, 2000, Cultural heritage of tribal societies-the Adis (vol-1), Omson Publication, New Delhi

Nyori,T, 1993, History and culture of Adis, Omson Publication, New Delhi

Osik,N.N, 2001, Nibo-Robo (a myth of Tani group of Arunachal Pradesh), Directorate of Art and Culture Govt. of Arunachal Pradesh, Naharlagun

Perme, Antoni, 2014, A study of beads among the Adi of Lower Dibang Valley, M.Phil Dissertation (unpublished), submitted to Rajiv Gandhi University, Rono Hills, Itanagar

Roy, Sachin, 1960, Aspects of Padam Minyong culture, Directorate of Research Govt. of Arunachal Pradesh, Itanagar

Tayeng, O, 2003, Folk tales of Adis, Mittal Publication, Delhi

Wojkowitz, R.N., 1952, Prehistoric beads from Tibet, Anthropological Institutes of Great Britain.

Chapter - 2

Syncretism in Social Science with special reference to the Noctes of Arunachal

Chandan Boruah

Syncretism is a very less used word in our daily lives, but in large, multi racial countries like India, USA, or European Union, without knowingly, people are becoming syncretic. In fact, syncretism defines as combination of two contradictory beliefs in social, cultural and political practices, and the reason and the study of syncretism holds an important place in social science. This article is based on the syncretism among the Noctes of Arunachal Pradesh as they identify themselves as Christians, yet, many of their tribal animistic beliefs are also continuing at the same time.

The Noctes of Tirap district, Arunachal Pradesh live in the Patkai mountain ranges of Northeastern India, bordering Myanmar. Noctes people are one of the major tribe of the state with around 30,000 populations out of the total population of Arunachal Pradesh (Census 2011). "Etymologically 'Nocte' means people living in an organized community. In the Ahom and early British periods Nocte tribes were referred to as Borduarias, Panduarias, Namsangia and Jaipurias. They had come into close contact with the people of Assam in the middle of the 19th Century (India netzone). Racially they belong to mongoloid race and "this tribe is believed to have migrated from Hukong Valley of Burma as they were attracted by the highland salt and pleasant climate of the Patkai Hills. The Noctes have cultural similarities with their neighboring Konyak Tribe of Nagaland such as the tradition of tattooing their faces and bodies, and like the fierce Konyaks, the Noctes also took part in headhunting" (Pastures; 2015).

"Noctes have been practicing an Indigenous Faith since time immemorial. It is based on Nature worship and upon a belief that the all powerful unseen God exists in the sky above. In the past, this indigenous

Faith had sobering effect on the people and was a unifying factor for the Noctes of different groups. The Indigenous Faith is known as Rangsom. It is believes in a Supreme Being known as Rangkathak. The God is called Jooban, Jongban and Huaba by various groups of Noctes" (Lowang; 2013).

Syncretism is a neutral term use to describe existence of two contradictory belief systems at a particular time within a particular group of people or society. 'Syncretism is found in different spheres of human life, especially society, culture and religion, in politics known as syncretic politics, and also in art and culture termed as eclecticism' (Taylor and Francis, 1998). Syncretism may takes place within a society due to some causes such as; culture contact, migration, conversion of religion and globalization.

The present study is to be carried out on syncretism with anthropological perspectives under Socio-Cultural anthropology among the Noctes of Tirap district; Arunachal Pradesh, India. Here in this paper, the primary objective is to document religious life of Noctes in Tirap district of Arunachal Pradesh whether their traditional animistic religion simply continues or it is syncretic in nature in course of time. Intensive fieldwork data are interpreted to fulfill the objective of research which is collected through observation and interview method. Data from secondary sources are also interpreted in the research.

Origin of the Noctes

Originally Noctes are followers of traditional animistic religion, but in course of time they have followed different religion and in the same time at present day they followed different religion in different areas or within a village itself but they are syncretic in nature.

Noctes in the past were the complete follower of their animistic religion and are famous for head hunting tradition. They were head hunters once and it was highly practiced among them. As a evidence of their head hunting tradition there are remains of human skulls and its fragments which are preserved in Pang (youth dormitory), in Tirap district of Arunachal Pradesh as Kheti basti and Namsang basti. Noctes nature worship is basically represented by worships of various stone and forest in different occasions present in particular area, which is practice among them from a long past till present.

Once Nocte were followers of Theravada Buddhism, which is dominant form of religion in Myanmar, where the Nocte migration is traced. "The 1961 census reported some Buddhist among the Noctes" (Das 1989). In

Past, Noctes came into contact of Hindu people from the plains of Assam, with home they traded salt and from the Assamese people they learnt the Assamese language and adapted the Hindu faith. "Noctes of Tirap profess the Mahapurushia form of vaishnavism propagated by Shrimanta Sankardeva in Assam" (Bose; 1997). The influence of Sankardevaa has bought them closer to the Hinddu once. "The first chief of Namsang and Borduria, was Known for his spirituality. The chief was baptized as "Narottam" by Sri Ram, Gukhai of Bareghor Satra. A place was named in honour of his name as Narottam nagar, where now the reputed institution, RK Mission is situated" (Dutta,1978). "Lotha Khonbao and his man joined the Vaishnava faith between 1669 and 1745 under the influence of Shri Ramdeva the vaishnava saint of Bali satra in Naharkatia. After his initiation Lotha was given the name Narottama".(Thakur,2006) Now some of the Noctes in Tirap district are Hindu and follow vaishnavism. But the ratio of vashnavism followers is very low. Due to negligence of some vaishnavait satas and leaders of Assam vaishnavism tend to vanished among them and today a few of them are vaishnavait. Due to lesser visit from the satra who taught them about vaishnavism the activities in the Namghars reduced and become less attracted towards the religion. Primeary data reveals that around 1972 Vaishnavism was spreaded by some representative and satradhikars of satras from Sasoni and Nagira area of Assam.

Now a day Christian religion is spreading very fast. Followers of Christian religion are in very much high ratio among the Noctes. Most of them have converted to Christianity specially those living in Khonsa and Borduria. Borduria is the only place in Arunachal Pradesh where Mother Theresa has visited. It was in the year 1993. There is the influence of great American missionary Miles Bronson who arrived in Tirap with the intension of spreading Christian religion. Now majority of the Nocte has converted to Christian religion. Baptist and Catholic are the most preferred form of Christian religion in the area but Baptist is in majority.

Syncretism in Nocte Religion

Noctes religion is very crystal clearly noticed that their religion that they never stuck to any kind of religion from the past till present. From their unknown past they were animist, having beliefs on a supreme god which is unseen believed to the creator of them and the environment. They have belief on both malevolent and benevolent god and spirits so they use to offer worships to them in the long past till present as still they do not mind about their present religion while performing their traditional animistic religious activities.

Megaliths which are found in various regions of Nocte inhabited area are also representative of their head hunting tradition. In certain festival occasion the practice of worshipping at megalith fields is still practice by them which involvs the local priest. Megalithic fields are also believed as a sacred place and therefore entry of outsider or commoners is prohibited in the megalith fields. This taboo is followed by Christian non Christian Nocte population. Priest hood is followed by the Noctes as to conduct various worships prevalent among them. Sometime the priest acts as a diviner and while some has both the personal separately. Vaishnavait Nocte deeply follows the virtue of Bareghoria Satra in addition to their animistic religion. in both past and present use to follow the religion mixed with their animistic faith. Among Vaishnavait Noctes follow the pattern of animistic devination in the name of their animistic supreme god and worships traditional deities. There are some remains of Namghar can be noticed in the Nocte inhabited area and some of them are still in good running condition. Vaishnavait Nocte use to pray at namghar regularly, namgharia referred to a person who regularly visits the namghor for worshiping. Religious performances is in some point has some differences from main stream of vaishnavite religion of Assam. Village Namsang is a good example having large number of Vaishnavait Noctes. This village has both Catholic and Baptist churches. Noctes whether animistic, Vaishnavait or Christian usually in festivals perform sacrificial ceremonies in both past and till present, which is lead by following of various taboos. Noctes posses beliefs in various malevolent spirits believed to be resides in trees and hills of the area and those can be manipulated my black magic. So it can be noticed that almost every house hold has put some skulls and bones of wild animal and feather of fowls at the main entrance of their houses. It is believed as these animal and fowl remains keep safe the house from entering such of malevolent sprits.

By the influence of Christian religion most of the population has adopted Christianity as their religion. Although people have adopted Christian religion Christianity is found to combine their basic elements of Tribal culture as well, which are normally not prescribed in the Bible. Followers of Christian religion also practices animal sacrifices follow traditional taboos associated with it. People often use to and drink prepare alcoholic braveries which is not prescribed norms of Baptistism. Noctes have not accepted Christian names for them and often follow animistic beliefs such as beliefs in Rango, worshipping of natural objects such as natural stones and Megaliths present in the area. "They often follow traditional norms during festival time besides they are Christian. Other malevolent and benevolent deities are also worshipped by offering of food and water given to the gods in order to apprise them". (Dutta,1978). Now the Noctes use to visit the church celebrate Christmas, follows the Christian norms and even they practice animistic beliefs and rituals. In case of marriage norms only tribe endogamy and clan exogamy is strictly followed, but religion never comes as verdict in case of marriage, they marriages takes place between non Christian and Christian mate. Christian Nocte use to grave their dead bodies with Christian norms, but offering of Nocte headgear and cloths of deceased person at the grave can be noticed, which is not a part of Christian norms.

Conclusion

Discussing religious life of Nocte people in Tirap, Arunachal Pradesh is not as simple to make a short conclusion, as it has passed through many conversions and different form of religion present among the Nocte. However it can be determined that, Nocte people do not follow a particular religion at present. As they have adopted different religion in their long past, now in their society followers of Animistic, vaishnavism and Christian can be found, where the ratio of Christian population is height among them. Within the same area and a village itself have followers of different religions.

Syncretism can be noticed in terms of religion among the Noctes of Tirap, Arunachal Pradesh. As many aspects of the animistic roots are still alive" among them it does not matter which particular religion they are following. People can be noticed following certain kind of beliefs which does not permitted by a religion which they presently following. Vaishnavite and Christian Noctes also follow traditional animistic religious beliefs and follow all traditional festivals and ceremonies. Thus religious life of Noctes can be observed and termed as sencretic in terms of religion as they follow one religion combining elements of their age old animistic religion with it.

References

Berndt, T. J. (2002). Friendship quality and social development. Current Directions in Psychological Science, 11, 7-10.

Bose M.L, (1997) History of Agrunachal Pradesh; Concept publishing Company, New delhi; Pp 35,37, 39.

Census of India, 2011.

Das Amrita. 2015. "The Nocte homeland trails"; The Hindu;

URL: http://www.thehindu.com/features/magazine/amrita-das-on-the-nocte-tribe-in-arunachal/article7720213.ece

Das Nava Kishor;(1989) Ethnic Identity, Ethnicity and Social Stratification in North East India; Inter-India Publications. Pp 38.

Greener Pastures; 2015. "Nocte Tribe of Arunachal Pradesh";

https://greenerpasturesind.wordpress.com/tag/nocte-tribe-2/

India netzone 2014. "Nocte Tribe, Arunachal Pradesh";

URL: http://www.indianetzone.com/8/nocte tribe.htm

Lowang, Wangpha. 2013. "Indigenous Faith & Culture of the Noctes", Heritage Explorer, Vol. XII. No.8, August 2013

Parul Chandra Dutta (1978). The Noctes. Directoriate of research, Govt. of Arunachal Pradesh. Pp.12,13,81.)

Taylor and Francis. 1998" "Brahman to Derrida: Victor Cousins eclectic syncretism"; Routledge Encyclopedia of Philosophy.

Thakur, Amarendra Kumar. (2006) Societ and Economy in North East India, Vol-2"Aspest of socio-political Formations in pre-Colonial Arunachal Pradesh"; Regency Publication, New Delhi; Pp. 171.

Chapter - 3

Changing aspects of fieldwork traditions in Anthropology

Dhritiman Sharma

Fieldwork is an integral part of anthropology, in physical, social and archeological anthropology. The fieldwork tradition started by Franz Boas in Baffin Island of Canada, where he conducted studies on the Inuits in 1881. Boas visited Baffin island as a geographer in that year, as he was working as a geographer at that moment. The non Western culture of Inuits attracted Boas and from direct contact, this may be considered as the first fieldwork in anthropology as Franz Boas is credited as the Father of Anthropology. Since then, fieldwork has become an integral part of anthropology. The fieldwork got accelerated by Malinowski when he conducted work in Polynesia among the Trobriand Islanders.

Fieldwork Traditions in Anthropology: Then and Now

100 years ago, when fieldwork started, the time was different. Now, the time has changed. Today, the anthropologists arrive their respective areas of fieldworks in well furnished cars, equipped with modern items. Moreover, the people, whom Franz Boas and Bronislaw Malinowski met, are also completely changed now. Anthropology is the holistic portrayal of man. It differs from other fields that study human society because anthropology is comparative, holistic and global. Traditionally, studying anthropology requires fieldwork in another society. They form personal relationships with local people as they study their lives. Cultural anthropology has two main scholarly components: ethnography and ethnology. Earlier, anthropologists focused on non-Western traditional people whose languages were not recorded in written form. These are the people whose communication is often direct and face-to-face, and whose knowledge about the past is primarily based on oral tradition. Even in

societies where writing exists, many of the things which interest the anthropologists are not documented. Thus, anthropologists have made a point of going to these places in person to see and experience people and their culture firsthand. This is what is known as field work.

Franz Boas is the pioneer of fieldwork traditions in anthropology. Boas took up geography as a way to explore his growing interest in the relationship between subjective experience and the objective world. At the time, German geographers were divided over the causes of cultural variation (Smith, 1991). Many argued that the physical environment was the principal determining factor, but others (notably Friedrich Ratzel) argued that the diffusion of ideas through human migration is more important. In 1883, encouraged by Theobald Fischer, Boas went to Baffin Island to conduct geographic research on the impact of the physical environment on native Inuit migrations. The first of many ethnographic field trips, Boas wrote his first monograph titled The Central Eskimo, which was published in 1888 in the 6th Annual Report from the Bureau of American Ethnology. Boas lived and worked closely with the Inuit peoples on Baffin Island, and he developed an abiding interest in the way people lived. (Boas, 1888: 399–670).

Anthropologist Frederic Ward Putnam, director and curator of the Peabody Museum at Harvard University, who had been appointed as head of the Department of Ethnology and Archeology for the Chicago Fair in 1892, chose Boas as his first assistant at Chicago to prepare for the 1893 World's Columbian Exposition or Chicago World's Fair, the 400th anniversary of Christopher Columbus's arrival in the Americas. (Truman, 1893). Boas had a chance to apply his approach to exhibits. Boas directed a team of about one hundred assistants, mandated to create anthropology and ethnology exhibits on the Indians of North America and South America that were living at the time Christopher Columbus arrived in America while searching for India. Putnam intended the World's Columbian Exposition to be a celebration of Columbus' voyage. Putnam argued that showing late 19th century Inuit and First Nations (then called Eskimo and Indians) "in their natural conditions of life" would provide a contrast and celebrate the four centuries of Western accomplishments since 1493. (Lorini, Alessandra (2003:1–25, archived from the original on 2016-01-27).

Franz Boas traveled north to gather ethnographic material for the Exposition. Boas had intended public science in creating exhibitions for the Exposition where visitors to the Midway could learn about other cultures. Boas arranged for fourteen Kwakiutl aboriginals from British Columbia to come and reside in a mock Kwakiutl village, where they could perform their daily tasks in context. Inuit were there with 12' long whips made of sealskin, wearing sealskin clothing and showing how adept they were in sealskin kayaks. His experience with the Exposition provided the first of a series of shocks to Franz Boas' faith in public anthropology. The visitors were not there to be educated. By 1916, Boas had come to recognize with a certain resignation that "the number of people in our country who are willing and able to enter into the modes of thought of other nations is altogether too small. The American who is cognizant only of his own standpoint sets himself up as arbiter of the world." (Boas, Franz (1945), "Race and Democratic Society", J. J. Augustin (1 ed.), New York A collection of 33 public addresses by the late Boas).

After the exposition, the ethnographic material collected formed the basis of the newly created Field Museum in Chicago with Boas as the curator of anthropology. (Stocking, 1982:354). He worked there until 1894, when he was replaced by archeologist William Henry Holmes.

In 1896, Boas was appointed Assistant Curator of Ethnology and Somatology of the American Museum of Natural History under Putnam. In 1897, he organized the Jesup North Pacific Expedition, a five-year-long field-study of the natives of the Pacific Northwest, whose ancestors had migrated across the Bering Strait from Siberia. He attempted to organize exhibits along contextual, rather than evolutionary, lines. He also developed a research program in line with his curatorial goals: describing his instructions to his students in terms of widening contexts of interpretation within a society, he explained that "... they get the specimens; they get explanations of the specimens; they get connected texts that partly refer to the specimens and partly to abstract things concerning the people; and they get grammatical information". These widening contexts of interpretation were abstracted into one context, the context in which the specimens, or assemblages of specimens, would be displayed: "... we want a collection arranged according to tribes, in order to teach the particular style of each group". His approach, however, brought him into conflict with the President of the Museum, Morris Jesup, and its director, Hermon Bumpus. By 1900 Boas had begun to retreat from American museum anthropology as a tool of education or reform. He resigned in 1905, never to work for a museum again.

In fact, from the brief biography of Franz Boas, it is clear that anthropological expeditions began in America with the work of Boas in Baffin Land and British Columbia, and were initiated in England shortly afterwards by Haddon of Cambridge, who led a band of scholars to conduct research in the Torres Straits region of the Pacific in 1898 and 1899. This expedition marked a turning-point in the history of social anthropology in Great Britain. Two important developments began to take place: anthropology became more and more a wholetime professional study and some field experience came to be regarded as an essential part of the training of its students. This early professional fieldwork had many weaknesses. They spent a short time among the people they studied and were ignorant of the languages of the people studied and their contacts with the people were superficial and casual. This did not permit deep investigation. Later studies of primitive societies became more intensive and illuminating. The most important of these include Radcliffe-Brown's study of the Andaman Islanders from 1906-1908. He was the first to investigate sociological theories in a primitive society and describe the social life of a people in such a way as to bring out clearly the significance in it for those theories. In the United States during the mid-nineteenth century, Lewis Henry Morgan showed that Iroquois behaviour and beliefs make sense if an outsider spends time learning about them, in context and through direct interactions and experience. He laid emphasis on direct observation and interactions. Participant Observation Bronislaw Malinowski, a pupil of Hobhouse, Westermarck and Seligman, carried field research a step further. He was a thorough field worker. He is credited with inventing a new approach to learning about culture while he was in the Trobriand Islands in the South Pacific during World War I. His approach is known as participant observation. He not only spent a longer period in studying a particular group of people, but was also the first to conduct his research through the native language. He studied the Trobriand Islanders between 1914 and 1918 and was the first to live throughout his work in the centre of native life. After the visit of Professor and Mrs. Seligman to the Anglo-Egyptian Sudan in 1909-1910, professional research in Africa started. Since then some of the important intensive studies were made which include Evans-Pritchard's study of the Azande of Anglo-Egyptian Sudan, Professor Schapera's account of the Bechuana, Professor Fortes's account of the Tallensi of the Gold Coast, Professor Nadel's account of the Nupe of Nigeria, Dr Kuper's Account of the Swazi, and Evans-Pritchard's account of the Nuer of the Anglo-Egyptian Sudan. Acculturation Studies Since the 1930s, the anthropologists have been aware that the number of traditional cultures is fast diminishing. In response some began studying asymmetrical culture contact, or acculturation. One of the first U.S. anthropologists to study acculturation was Margaret Mead in her 1932 fieldwork among the Omaha Indians of Nebraska. She focused in that research, on community breakdown and cultural disintegration of this traditional American Indian tribe. In the course of 20th century, numerous other anthropologists carried out acculturation studies in Asia, Africa, Australia, Oceania, the Americas, and even in parts of Europe itself. Applied Anthropology Acculturation studies in turn gave rise to applied anthropology.

In 1937, an anthropological research institute was set up by the British government in Zambia to study the impact of international markets on Central Africa's traditional societies. In the next decade anthropologists worked on a number of problem-oriented studies throughout Africa. North America also faced similar problems and so the U.S. Bureau of Indian Affairs (BIA) established an applied anthropology branch in the mid-1930s. Apart from studying the problems of acculturation, the bureau aimed to identify practical culturally appropriate ways for the U.S. government to introduce social and economic development programmes to reduce poverty, promote literacy, and solve a host of other problems on the reservations. In 1941, the now international Society for Applied Anthropology was founded at Harvard University to promote scientific investigation of the principles controlling the relations of human beings to one another and the encouragement of their wide application. At present, a large number of professionally trained anthropologists are specialized in applied research and are active at numerous areas in every corner of the world. Long-distance anthropological studies During World War II (1939-1945) and the early years of the Cold War, some anthropologists diverted their focus from small-scale societies to modern state societies. Their aim was to discern basic personality traits shared by majority of the people in modern state societies. A number of U.S.and British anthropologists became involved in a wartime government programme of 'national character' studies. Such studies helped to understand better and deal with the newly declared enemy states of Japan and Germany (in World War II) and later Russia and others. During wartime on-location ethnographic fieldwork was not possible in enemy societies and in other foreign countries. Therefore, Mead, Ruth Benedict, and other anthropologists developed innovative techniques. According to them, culture at a distance can be studied through analysis of newspapers, literature, photographs, and popular films. They also collected information through structured interviews with immigrants and refugees from the enemy nations, as well as foreigners from other countries.

Study of Contemporary State Societies Anthropological research began to focus on contemporary state societies. They believed that in addition to small-scale societies, they should also study the complex, large-scale societies organized in political states, like that of modern France or the

United States. During the years of the Great Depression (1930s), several anthropologists already worked in their own countries studying factories, farming communities and suburban neighbourhoods. The U.S. anthropologist, Hortense Powder maker, did her first major ethnographic fieldwork among the Melanesians in the southern Pacific. In the 1930s, after returning to the United States, she researched a racially segregated town in Mississippi. She focused during the next decade on combating dominant society's racism against African Americans and other ethnic minorities. She noticed the importance of the mass media in shaping people's worldviews and focused on the domestic film industry and did a year of fieldwork in Hollywood (1946-1947). During this period, several anthropologists were busy on other kinds of studies in large-scale societies. Margaret Mead and Ruth Benedict, for instance, were of the view that governments and colonial administrations, as well as new global institutions such as the United Nations (founded in 1945), could and should get benefit from anthropological insights. They initiated a team project in comparative research on contemporary cultures based at Columbia University in New York (1947-1952). Swiss anthropologist, Alfred Metraux put together an international team of U.S., French, and Brazilian researchers to study contemporary race relations in South American country, Brazil in 1950. The project was sponsored by UNESCO and it was part of the UN's global campaign against racial prejudice and discrimination. U.S. anthropologist Julian Steward, in 1956 and 1957, supervised an anthropological research team in developing countries such as Kenya, Nigeria, Peru, Mexico, Japan, Burma, Malaya, and Indonesia. Their purpose was to study the comparative impact of industrialization and urbanization upon these different populations. Similar projects were launched by other anthropologists in other parts of the world. Peasant Studies While anthropologists began to widen their knowledge regarding the complex societies, some of them started to concentrate on peasant communities. Peasantry represents the largest social category and anthropological studies of these rural populations in Latin America, Africa, Asia, and elsewhere are considered significant. Robert Redfield, Eric Wolf, Raymond Firth and others made significant contributions in this regard.

Advocacy Anthropology by the 1960s, political unrest made fieldwork difficult in many parts of the world. Europ ean colonial powers had lost almost all of their overseas territorial possessions. So, a large number of anthropologists investigated important issues of culture change and conflicts inside Europe and North America. Some of these issues involve immigrants and refugees who come from places where anthropologists have conducted research. Some anthropologists have gone a step further by helping them adjust to their new circumstances. Others have become advocates for peasant communities, ethnic or religious minorities, or indigenous groups struggling to hold onto their ancestral lands, natural resources, and customary ways of life. One of the first anthropological research projects explicitly addressing the quest for social justice and cultural survival took place among the Fox Indians (North American Indian Community) on their reservation in the state of Iowa (1948-1959). U.S. anthropologist, Sol Tax, based on long-term fieldwork with this community, challenged government-sponsored applied anthropological research projects. He instead proposed that researchers work directly with disadvantaged, exploited, and oppressed communities and help identify and solve their own problems. Nowadays, most anthropologists committed to community-based and politically involved research refer to their work as advocacy anthropology. For over three decades, U.S.anthropologist Robert Hitchcock has practised advocacy anthropology. He has focused primarily on land rights, as well as the social, economic, and cultural rights of indigenous people in southern Africa, especially Bushmen groups in Botswana. Studying up The term "study up" was coined by U.S.anthropologist Laura Nader. She has urged anthropologists to lay emphasis on Western elites, government bureaucracies, global corporations, philanthropic foundations, media empires, business clubs, and so on. But to do participant observation in these well-guarded circles is a formidable challenge. Multi-sited research and globalization In recent times as a result of globalization and mass communication very few cultures seem to remain isolated. Cultural anthropologists have devised new research methods so that they can study larger-scale cultures, global-local connections, and rapid cultural change. Globalization has given rise to a new trend in anthropological research, known as multi-sited research. It is fieldwork conducted on a topic in more than one location. This type of research involves the investigation and documentation of people and cultures embedded in the larger structures of a globalizing world, utilizing a range of methods in various locations of time and space. A recent work on a diasporic ethnic group on the transnational Chinese identities was conducted by Chinese American anthropologist Andrea Louie. Her fieldwork carried her to an array of locations in San Francisco, Hong Kong, and southern China. Also emerging in multi-sited ethnography are greater interdisciplinary approaches to fieldwork, bringing in theoretical ideas and research methods from cultural studies, media studies, and mass communication, among others.

However, in the fast-changing, globalizing world of the present century, core ethnographic research methods developed about a century ago, continue to be relevant. Pilot survey refers to studies done before conducting a larger study. In those areas where literature seems to be inadequate, pilot study may be launched as a preliminary step to the formulation of a schedule. All that can be formulated at this stage is an interview guide. Thus the researcher interviews in the field in a very nondirective fashion. The questions are structured and controlled only by dealing with these general areas which he has reason to think are important. During this kind of flexible interviewing, he tries to follow up every promising lead which may appear, as to meaning of phrases, embarrassing areas of inquiry, differences of response to what seems to be the same question, new areas of subject matter, etc. The researcher is clarifying and formulating hypotheses for a subsequent study. He is not putting neat hypotheses to the test at this stage. He is not only uncertain as to the materials he wants to inquire about, but he may even be uncertain as to whom he wishes to interview. This stage does not usually warrant a formal sampling design, but the student must be sure that he interviews a wide variety of the various types making up the final sample to be studied. Moreover, he must be alert to field-sampling problems which may warn him to take precautions at the stage of formal sampling design. The results of these intensive interviews must then be written up and carefully analyzed, for they furnish the logical basis upon which the subsequent questionnaire will be used. If well done and thoroughly exploited, the pilot study will usually prove to be a substantial saver of time and effort by helping to avoid erroneous and insignificant hypotheses. In 1999, Katherine Browne, Carla Freeman, and Zobeida Bonilla began a comparative ethnographic study of women entrepreneurs in Martinique, Barbados, and Puerto Rico—that is, in the French,English,and Spanish-speaking Caribbean. This is a large multi-site, where it pays to spend time on pilot research. Each member of the team did 30-indepth interviews with women who were engaged in a wide range of enterprises, who were of different ages and who came from one-and two-parent homes. This helped the team develop their research instruments and provided the baseline for the larger project (Browne 2001).

In large-scale studies, preliminary pilot studies are essential in order to see flaws and handicaps which might be encountered in the full-scale study. Such foreshadowing of difficulties requires utmost care in the execution of the preliminary study. If the pilot study does not succeed in disclosing the significant difficulties which should be guarded against, the full-scale study modeled on it may perpetuate and even augment these difficulties. Conclusion Fieldwork has come a long way in anthropology from the time of armchair anthropologists. Topics have changed, as have techniques of data gathering and data analysis. Today, anthropological fieldwork takes place not only in small-scale communities in distant corners of the world, but also in modern urban neighborhoods in industrial or postindustrial societies. Anthropologists can be found doing fieldwork in a wide range of places and within a host of diverse groups, including transnational corporations, international migrant workers, and people scattered and dispersed because of wars, famines, poverty, or persecution. New techniques continue to develop in response to changing times. But the hallmarks of anthropology, that is, holistic research through fieldwork with participant observation is still a valued and productive tradition. Fieldwork Tradition in Anthropology and Pilot Survey Introduction Anthropology is the holistic portrayal of man. It differs from other fields that study human society because anthropology is comparative, holistic and global. Traditionally, studying anthropology requires fieldwork in another society. They form personal relationships with local people as they study their lives. Cultural anthropology has two main scholarly components: ethnography and ethnology. Earlier, anthropologists focused on non-Western traditional people whose languages were not recorded in written form. These are the people whose communication is often direct and face-to-face, and whose knowledge about the past is primarily based on oral tradition. Even in societies where writing exists, many of the things which interest the anthropologists are not documented. Thus, anthropologists have made a point of going to these places in person to see and experience people and their culture firsthand. This is what is known as field work. In this unit we will discuss in brief the fieldwork tradition in anthropology and importance of pilot survey. Historical background Early cultural anthropologists conducted research by sitting at home in their library and reading reports about other cultures written by travelers, missionaries, and explorers. These early thinkers never visited the places they wrote about and had no direct experience with the people whose customs they discussed. During the heyday of colonialism (1870s-1950s) when many European anthropologists focused on the study of traditional peoples and their cultures in the colonies overseas, cultural anthropology really emerged. Anthropological expeditions began in America with the work of Boas in Baffin Land and British Columbia, and were initiated in England shortly afterwards by Haddon of Cambridge, who led a band of scholars to conduct research in the Torres Straits region of the Pacific in 1898 and 1899. This expedition marked a turning-point in the history of social anthropology in Great Britain. Two important developments began to take place: anthropology became more and more a wholetime professional study and some field experience came to be regarded as an essential part of the training of its students. This early professional fieldwork had many weaknesses. They spent a short time among the people they studied and were ignorant of the languages of the people studied and their contacts with the people were superficial and casual. This did not permit deep investigation.

Later studies of primitive societies became more intensive and illuminating. The most important of these include Radcliffe-Brown's study of the Andaman Islanders from 1906-1908. He was the first to investigate sociological theories in a primitive society and describe the social life of a people in such a way as to bring out clearly the significance in it for those theories. In the United States during the mid-nineteenth century, Lewis Henry Morgan showed that Iroquois behaviour and beliefs make sense if an outsider spends time learning about them, in context and through direct interactions and experience. He laid emphasis on direct observation and interactions. Participant Observation Bronislaw Malinowski, a pupil of Hobhouse, Westermarck and Seligman, carried field research a step further. He was a thorough field worker. He is credited with inventing a new approach to learning about culture while he was in the Trobriand Islands in the South Pacific during World War I. His approach is known as participant observation. He not only spent a longer period in studying a particular group of people, but was also the first to conduct his research through the native language. He studied the Trobriand Islanders between 1914 and 1918 and was the first to live throughout his work in the centre of native life. After the visit of Professor and Mrs. Seligman to the Anglo-Egyptian Sudan in 1909-1910, professional research in Africa started. Since then some of the important intensive studies were made which include Evans-Pritchard's study of the Azande of Anglo-Egyptian Sudan, Professor Schapera's account of the Bechuana, Professor Fortes's account of the Tallensi of the Gold Coast, Professor Nadel's account of the Nupe of Nigeria, Dr Kuper's Account of the Swazi, and Evans-Pritchard's account of the Nuer of the Anglo-Egyptian Sudan. Acculturation Studies Since the 1930s, the anthropologists have been aware that the number of traditional cultures is fast diminishing. In response some began studying asymmetrical (sharply uneven) culture contact, or acculturation. One of the first U.S. anthropologists to study acculturation was Margaret Mead in her 1932 fieldwork among the Omaha Indians of Nebraska. She focused in that research, on community breakdown and cultural disintegration of this traditional American Indian tribe. In the course of 20th century, numerous other anthropologists carried out acculturation studies in Asia, Africa, Australia, Oceania, the Americas, and even in parts of Europe itself. Applied Anthropology Acculturation studies in turn gave rise to applied anthropology.

In 1937, an anthropological research institute was set up by the British government in Zambia to study the impact of international markets on Central Africa's traditional societies. In the next decade anthropologists worked on a number of problem-oriented studies throughout Africa. North America also faced similar problems and so the U.S.Bureau of Indian Affairs (BIA) established an applied anthropology branch in the mid-1930s. Apart from studying the problems of acculturation, the bureau aimed to identify practical culturally appropriate ways for the U.S. government to introduce social and economic development programmes to reduce poverty, promote literacy, and solve a host of other problems on the reservations. In 1941, the now international Society for Applied Anthropology was founded at Harvard University to promote scientific investigation of the principles controlling the relations of human beings to one another and the encouragement of their wide application. At present, a large number of professionally trained anthropologists are specialized in applied research and are active at numerous areas in every corner of the world. Long-distance anthropological studies During World War II (1939-1945) and the early years of the Cold War, some anthropologists diverted their focus from small-scale societies to modern state societies. Their aim was to discern basic personality traits shared by majority of the people in modern state societies. A number of U.S.and British anthropologists became involved in a wartime government programme of 'national character' studies. Such studies helped to understand better and deal with the newly declared enemy states of Japan and Germany (in World War II) and later Russia and others. During wartime on-location ethnographic fieldwork was not possible in enemy societies and in other foreign countries. Therefore, Mead, Ruth Benedict, and other anthropologists developed innovative techniques. According to them, culture at a distance can be studied through analysis of newspapers, literature, photographs, and popular films. They also collected information through structured interviews with immigrants and refugees from the enemy nations, as well as foreigners from other countries.

Study of Contemporary State Societies Anthropological research began to focus on contemporary state societies. They believed that in addition to small-scale societies, they should also study the complex, large-scale societies organized in political states, like that of modern France or the United States. During the years of the Great Depression (1930s), several anthropologists already worked in their own countries studying factories, farming communities and suburban neighbourhoods. The U.S. anthropologist, Hortense Powdermaker, did her first major ethnographic fieldwork among the Melanesians in the southern Pacific. In the 1930s, after returning to the United States, she researched a racially segregated town in Mississippi. She focused during the next decade on combating dominant society's racism against African Americans and other ethnic minorities. She noticed the importance of the mass media in shaping people's worldviews and focused on the domestic film industry and did a year of fieldwork in Hollywood (1946-1947). During this period, several anthropologists were busy on other kinds of studies in large-scale societies. Margaret Mead and Ruth Benedict, for instance, were of the view that governments and colonial administrations, as well as new global institutions such as the United Nations (founded in 1945), could and should get benefit from anthropological insights. They initiated a team project in comparative research on contemporary cultures based at Columbia University in New York (1947-1952). Swiss anthropologist, Alfred Metraux put together an international team of U.S., French, and Brazilian researchers to study contemporary race relations in South American country, Brazil in 1950. The project was sponsored by UNESCO and it was part of the UN's global campaign against racial prejudice and discrimination. U.S. anthropologist Julian Steward, in 1956 and 1957, supervised an anthropological research team in developing countries such as Kenya, Nigeria, Peru, Mexico, Japan, Burma, Malaya, and Indonesia. Their purpose was to study the comparative impact of industrialization and urbanization upon these different populations. Similar projects were launched by other anthropologists in other parts of the world.

Peasant Studies While anthropologists began to widen their knowledge regarding the complex societies, some of them started to concentrate on peasant communities. Peasantry represents the largest social category and anthropological studies of these rural populations in Latin America, Africa, Asia, and elsewhere are considered significant. Robert Redfield, Eric Wolf, Raymond Firth and others made significant contributions in this regard. Advocacy Anthropology By the 1960s, political unrest made fieldwork difficult in many parts of the world. Europ ean colonial powers had lost almost all of their overseas territorial possessions. So, a large number of anthropologists investigated important issues of culture change and conflicts inside Europe and North America. Some of these issues involve immigrants and refugees who come from places where anthropologists have conducted research. Some anthropologists have gone a step further by helping them adjust to their new circumstances. Others have become advocates for peasant communities, ethnic or religious minorities, or indigenous groups struggling to hold onto their ancestral lands, natural resources, and customary ways of life. One of the first anthropological research projects explicitly addressing the quest for social justice and cultural survival took place among the Fox Indians (North American Indian Community) on their reservation in the state of Iowa (1948-1959). U.S. anthropologist, Sol Tax, based on long-term fieldwork with this community, challenged government-sponsored applied anthropological research projects. He instead proposed that researchers work directly with disadvantaged, exploited, and oppressed communities and help identify and solve their own problems.

Nowadays, most anthropologists committed to community-based and politically involved research refer to their work as advocacy anthropology. For over three decades, U.S.anthropologist Robert Hitchcock has practised advocacy anthropology. He has focused primarily on land rights, as well as the social, economic, and cultural rights of indigenous people in southern Africa, especially Bushmen groups in Botswana. Studying up The term "study up" was coined by U.S.anthropologist Laura Nader. She has urged anthropologists to lay emphasis on Western elites, government bureaucracies, global corporations, philanthropic foundations, media empires, business clubs, and so on. But to do participant observation in these well-guarded circles is a formidable challenge. Multi-sited research and globalization In recent times as a result of globalization and mass communication very few cultures seem to remain isolated. Cultural anthropologists have devised new research methods so that they can study larger-scale cultures, global-local connections, and rapid cultural change. Globalization has given rise to a new trend in anthropological research, known as multi-sited research. It is fieldwork conducted on a topic in more than one location. This type of research involves the investigation and documentation of people and cultures embedded in the larger structures of a globalizing world, utilizing a range of methods in various locations of time and space. A recent work on a diasporic ethnic group on the transnational Chinese identities was conducted by Chinese American anthropologist Andrea Louie. Her fieldwork carried her to an array of locations in San Francisco, Hong Kong, and southern China. Also emerging in multi-sited ethnography are greater interdisciplinary approaches to fieldwork, bringing in theoretical ideas and research methods from cultural studies, media studies, and mass communication, among others. However, in the fast-changing, globalizing world of the present century, core ethnographic research methods developed about a century ago, continue to be relevant. Pilot survey refers to studies done before conducting a larger study. In those areas where literature seems to be inadequate, pilot study may be launched as a preliminary step to the formulation of a schedule. All that can be formulated at this stage is an interview guide. Thus the researcher interviews in the field in a very nondirective fashion. The questions are structured and controlled only by dealing with these general areas which he has reason to think are important. During this kind of flexible interviewing, he tries to follow up every promising lead which may appear, as to meaning of phrases, embarrassing areas of inquiry, differences of response to what seems to be the same question, new areas of subject matter, etc. The researcher is clarifying and formulating hypotheses for a subsequent study. He is not putting neat hypotheses to the test at this stage. He is not only uncertain as to the materials he wants to inquire about, but he may even be uncertain as to whom he wishes to interview. This stage does not usually warrant a formal sampling design, but the student must be sure that he interviews a wide variety of the various types making up the final sample to be studied. Moreover, he must be alert to field-sampling problems which may warn him to take precautions at the stage of formal sampling design. The results of these intensive interviews must then be written up and carefully analyzed, for they furnish the logical basis upon which the subsequent questionnaire will be used. If well done and thoroughly exploited, the pilot study will usually prove to be a substantial saver of time and effort by helping to avoid erroneous and insignificant hypotheses.

In 1999, Katherine Browne, Carla Freeman, and Zobeida Bonilla began a comparative ethnographic study of women entrepreneurs in Martinique, Barbados, and Puerto Rico—that is, in the French,English,and Spanish-speaking Caribbean. This is a large multi-site, where it pays to spend time on pilot research. Each member of the team did 30-indepth interviews with women who were engaged in a wide range of enterprises, who were of different ages and who came from one-and two-parent homes. This helped the team develop their research instruments and provided the baseline for the larger project (Browne 2001). In large-scale studies, preliminary pilot studies are essential in order to see flaws and handicaps which might be encountered in the full-scale study. Such foreshadowing of difficulties requires utmost care in the execution of the preliminary study. If the pilot study does not succeed in disclosing the significant difficulties which should be guarded against, the full-scale study modeled on it may perpetuate and even augment these difficulties.

Fieldwork has come a long way in anthropology from the time of armchair anthropologists. Topics have changed, as have techniques of data gathering and data analysis. Today, anthropological fieldwork takes place not only in small-scale communities in distant corners of the world, but also in modern urban neighborhoods in industrial or postindustrial societies. Anthropologists can be found doing fieldwork in a wide range of places and within a host of diverse groups, including transnational corporations, international migrant workers, and people scattered and dispersed because of wars, famines, poverty, or persecution. New techniques continue to develop in response to changing times. But the hallmarks of anthropology, that is, holistic research through fieldwork with participant observation is still a valued and productive tradition (http://eacharya.inflibnet.ac.in/data-server/eacharya-documents/5717528c8ae36ce69422587d INFIEP 304/172/ET/304-172-ET-V1-S1 file1.pdf).

Changes: Should we Require?

Nowhere it is mentioned, what should be the duration of fieldwork. In this regard, we are always in dilemma what to do as fieldwork is mostly used to train up the students of Higher Secondary, Graduate and Post Graduate students. In North East India, fieldwork tradition is inspired by Calcutta University being the nearest and many of our earlier students often got the BA and MA degree from Calcutta University. In fact, CU is famous for its long duration fieldwork of 30 days in MA course, covering all the 3 aspects of social anthropology (ethnographic fieldwork), physical anthropology and archeological anthropology respectively (personal communication with Professor Sarit Kumar Chaudhuri). Time has changed, and that long duration of fieldwork was reduced to 21 days when I was enrolled as MA student in 2002. In fact, I was very lucky to get my fieldwork training under 5 notable anthropologists of North East India, Professor Tiluttoma Barua and Professor Jonali Devi of Cotton College, Guwahati in 1999 as BA student, while doing the 2nd fieldwork under Professor Lanu Devi in 2000. Then in 2002, in MA, I got the chance to do my fieldwork under the supervision of Professor Birinchi Kumar Medhi and Professor Mini Bhattacharya, and finally, due to my specialization in archeological anthropology, I got the chance to do my fieldwork under Professor Abdullah Ali Ashraf and Dr Shankar Kumar Roy, then curator of the Department of Anthropology. Hence, I will narrate my experience about fieldwork in different phases of my life and also going through the experiences in both long and short term durations, as student and now as faculty.

Duration of Fieldwork Depending on Works: Graduation to Phd

On the basis of the specialization in anthropology, three types of fieldworks are there. This is more common once the students choose specialization either in cultural anthropology, physical anthropology or archeology. From graduation till post graduation, normally, ethnographic fieldwork is taught. Hence, I am stressing on the ethnographic fieldwork in this article. This fieldwork may be completed in short duration if the time is utilized in a proper way, even as low as in 3 to 5 days too in entry level. In terms of verification and nature of aptitude of the students, a period of one week is sufficient in modern days now. However, in terms of physical anthropology, where a large number of data are required for verification in terms physical studies and human anatomy of a particular race, time is usually increased, with a minimum period of 10 days. Similarly, in archeology fieldwork, it depends on the nature of the work. If the fieldwork requires excavation, then depending on the nature of excavation, the duration of fieldwork may increase from 7 days to 15 days.

Graduate students get the first idea of fieldwork while visiting an area, normally to a village. They have to conduct the fieldwork by staying in the area, or by going everyday from their nearby college. At this stage, for teenaged boys and girls, first obstacle comes at the point of rapport establishment with the elderly people of the village, as at this stage, students are usually shy, and asking about various dimensions of life, especially topics related to marriage, family, childcare are little bit difficult for them. Hence, first challenge, teachers get to make them prepare about speaking freely with the elders to collect the data. In fact, overnight, nobody can master such art, but slowly, if students concentrate to ask questions to the people, the concept of rapport establishment as the first goal is achieved well at this stage. Another reality is that a vast majority of students conclude their study in graduate level, and opt for other professional courses like MBA, or prepare for jobs. Hence, at this stage, a simple ethnographic data collection as part of the graduate training within a period of 3-7 days is enough in colleges in anthropology fieldwork course.

The next stage after graduation is post graduation. At this stage, students become matured adults, and some new stress of training may be implemented on them, in the curriculum, depending on their aptitude. However, out of the post graduate students batch, not everyone is going to continue in research line, and as per practical uses in the universities, it has been observed that, every batch produces maximum 2 or 3 JRFs or NET qualified students. These NET qualified students normally continue in PhD or M Phil, and in fact, the absolute rigorous training for them is mandatory. This is the reason, why now a days, M Phil and PhD coursework programs have research methodology papers, and they need to prepare themselves for long duration fieldwork within their 2 years M Phil program and 3-5 years long PhD programs. Hence, in MA level also, an extension of the BA fieldwork is required, which is in the period of 7 to 15 days, or 10 days in average may be taken. However, as graduate students already taken to the fieldwork by their respective teachers, post graduate students should be given the task of doing the fieldwork by themselves as they are normally doing at present in 3rd and 4th semester. The mandatory fieldwork in 1st or 2nd semester may be omitted at present, as anthropology graduates are already been trained up in colleges under their experienced faculties.

M Phil and PhD are the final stages of research in academics. Uring the period of 2 years in M Phil and 3-5 years in PhD, students can apply participant observation techniques properly by staying in a village upto 1 year, without a break. Such long term fieldworks are possible only during the time such research, and otherwise during the time of student life, all things are actually part of training.

Conclusion

Academic activities are subject to change. What was practiced 100 years ago are still relevant, but changes are required today. Based on the works of Franz Boas and Bronislaw Malinowski, we have to accelerate the fieldwork traditions with change. If we never change, the tradition will disappear with time, if the process becomes outdated. That's why, we need to minimize the duration of fieldwork in training programs at present.

References

Smith, W. D. (1991), Politics and the sciences of culture in Germany. 1840–1920, New York: Oxford University Press, ISBN 9780195362275.

Boas, Franz (1888), "The Central Eskimo", Smithsonian Institution via Gutenberg, Sixth Annual Report of the Bureau of Ethnology to the Secretary of the Smithsonian Institution, 1884-1885, Government Printing Office, Washington, pp. 399–670, retrieved 13 January 2015.

Cole, Herbert, ed. (1983), Franz Boas' Baffin Island Letter-Diary, 1883–1884

Cole, Douglas 1983 "The Value of a Person Lies in His Herzensbildung": Franz Boas's Baffin Island Letter-Diay, 1883–1884. In Observers Observed: Essays on Ethnographic Fieldwork. George W. Stocking Jr., ed. pp. 13–52. Madison: University of Wisconsin Press.

Cole, Douglas. 1999/ Franz Boas: The Early Years. 1858–1906. Seattle: University of Washington Press.

Truman, Benjamin (1893). History of the World's Fair: Being a Complete and Authentic Description of the Columbian Exposition From Its Inception. Philadelphia, PA: J. W. Keller & Co.

"Bird's-Eye View of the World's Columbian Exposition, Chicago, 1893". World Digital Library. 1893. Retrieved 2013-07-17.

Lorini, Alessandra (2003), "Alice Fletcher and the Search for Women's Public Recognition in Professionalizing American Anthropology", Cromohs, Florence, Italy, 8, pp. 1–25, archived from the original on 2016-01-27.

Boas, Franz (1945), "Race and Democratic Society", J. J. Augustin (1 ed.), New YorkA collection of 33 public addresses by the late Boas.

http://eacharya.inflibnet.ac.in/data-server/eacharya documents/5717528c 8ae36ce69422587d INFIEP 304/172/ET/304-172-ET-V1-S1 file1.pdf).

Chapter - 4

Tribal development and the Irulas

E Tamil Selvan

India is home for tribal population after Africa .They are scattered all over states. The 83 million tribal peoples of India make up 8 per cent of the country's total population, and belong to 461 officially recognized groups. The largest concentrations of indigenous peoples are found in the seven states of north-east India, and the so called "central tribal belt" stretching from Rajasthan to West Bengal. Rath concludes that 'the mainstream development model has limited impact on the people living at the periphery, specifically on tribes' a failure all the more tragic given that it is precisely these marginalized citizens who have been the target of elaborate tribal welfare programmes (Mark 2008).

Most of tribes in India land play a major role to full fill their needs in terms of subsistence. The livelihood depends on land and allied activities. Alienation of land from tribal is one major issues faced by tribal communities.

Planning commission of India also carried over issues on land alienation and indebtness among tribals in Tamilnadu , Kerala and Karnataka. In Kerala human development report under the project with UNDP and planning commission, the report will reflect the land is lost because of settlers and encroachers. Section 4(5) The Scheduled Tribes and Other Traditional Forest Dwellers (Recognition of Forest Rights) Act, 2006 provides that no member of a forest-dwelling Scheduled Tribe or other traditional forest dweller shall be evicted or removed from land under his occupation until the recognition and verification procedure for settlement of forest rights is complete. (IWGIA – The Indigenous World – 2016).

Tribes are denied to access resources in forest due to the implementation of Forest Right Act 2006 and wild life protection act1972. Access is very limited to collect minor forest products. There is a person who as middle men who exploited tribes.

Tribal Scenario in Tamil Nadu

Saravanan discusses the tribal economy of Tamil Nadu from 1947 to 2000 and shows how the position of tribes as cultivators has over time been downgraded to that of agricultural labourers. (Mark 2008).

The tribal situation in Tamilnadu poses peculiar problems of development, not encountered in other areas. The peculiarities can be broadly summed up as geographical, demographic, socio-cultural and exploitative (cited page no 4 Perumal, Padmanaban1986).

In general the Government Tamilnadu has accepted the statistics provided by the Centre and its various commissions with regard to the problem of the tribal's till 1970, and in that year the state governmenth as appointed for the first time the Karthikeyan Commission with wide terms of reference to assess the overall tribal situation in Tamilnadu (cited p.no6 Perumal and Padmanaban).

"The economy of the tribals in forest areas is dependent on the forest resources" - Policy Note on Forest Department 1999-2000 (cited). Forest is a major resource for the survival of tribes. They are not trained any other skills to work in different occupations.

In early 2000, a member of the Tamilnadu Human Rights Commission had claimed that the Rs. 400 crores allocated for tribal welfare had not been spent and that many tribal's had been denied their community certificates.(Tamilnadu Social Development report 2000). Denying community certificate for tribes directly affect their children to pursue higher education.

Tribals in Tamilnadu have for long been demanding that their areas should be included under the Fifth Schedule of the Constitution. Self-rule, as articulated by the Bhuria Committee 1996 Report offers a clearly viable possibility for empowering the dalits. Self-rule should pave the way for the tribal communities to acquire the power to own and manage the resources of the forests and also to govern their own institutions.(Tamilnadu social development report 2000).

Anthropology and Development

The key factor responsible for the ascendance of anthropology in development circles is the increasingly large numbers of academic social scientists keen to demonstrate the policy relevance and maximize the beneficial effects of their research contributions .The number of such academics trying to understand and provide better solutions to crucial human problems relating to the interactions among culture, the environment, and development is expected to continue to increase in the decades ahead (cited p.no 2 Paiment Napa bulletin 27, 2007).

The anthropology of development: namely, the crucial importance of detailed ethnographic work on the production and transformation of the social practices of development and, hence, the need for ethnography in shaping development policies. (cited Paiement Napa bulletin 272007).

Anthropology of development seeks to understand development in terms of structural process as well as in terms of interaction between various actors and systems of knowledge. (cited Bakker et. al 2017).

The inclusion of disadvantaged and marginalised groups has been central element throughout the history of anthropological approaches to development.(Bakker et. al).

Development anthropology is scientific research with significant applications within the development project cycle. Its objective is to enhance benefits and mitigate negative consequences for the human communities involved in and affected by development efforts. Development anthropologists are in-volved in development projects in a variety of ways, the specific roles being determined in part by the particularst age in the life cycle of the project. (Partridge 1984).

Statement of the Problem

Whether tribal developmental intervention program will effectively impact tribes of irula in nilgris district through different agencies?

Area of Study and Community

Irula is one of the scheduled tribes in Tamil Nadu that live in the Nilgris district. They are mostly concentrated in Kotagiri, Coonur, Ooty and Gudalur Taluk. Earlier Irula tribes were hunters and gatherers. Now their main occupation is agriculture. The purpose of the paper is to study about the Irula people who are living in the Kurumbarpallam settlement who are surrounded by adjoining Irula settlements like Thakkal, Thotulingi, Kurumbarpadi and Kovilpati.

This paper is mainly focused on the livelihood conditions, the transition from agriculture to working as wage laborers in resorts and guest house in the Bokkapuram and the nearby places where around 20 guest houses are located. It addresses the issues on lack of employment, social security, poor conditions of housing, polluted drinking water, lack of communication and development of these marginalized people.

Methodology

Primary data is gathered through intensive field work. The researcher did one month field work November month 2016. Data is gathered through participation observation and socio economic details are collected semi structured interview schedule Irulas. Case study method adopted to understand the development programmes. Key informants method is used to collect the data from those who gained from the beneficial and developmental schemes. Secondary data is collected based on journals, reports, Magazines, etc.

Findings & Discussion

The Irula men works as a labor doing activities like gardening, making tents, arrange trekking, bird watching inside the forest for the guests and serve them providing necessary facilities. The women are engaged in cleaning the rooms; wash the clothes, providing assistance in cooking and other activities.

Livelihood

Irula is one of the Particularly Vulnerable Tribal Groups in Nilgris Tamil Nadu. The remaining tribal groups are Toda, Kota, Paniyan, Kattunaiyaken and Kurumbas. These six PVTGs have its distinct cultural practice in term of their social institutions, occupation, religion, and political system. They all are integrated with inter tribal relationship to others. Irulas livelihood mainly depends on forest and natural resources available in the habitat. They practice agriculture using simple technology. They cultivate millet and horticultural crops but seldom tea or coffee in the lands. Women sometimes engage in basket making helped by some cooperative societies. In addition they are rearing cow, buffalo, goat, sheep and allied activities. The settlements in the forest are reduced due to the restriction of forest department to access the resources. Basic needs and amenities like water, health, education, housing, and roads are not fulfilled.

Male and Female Population

The total member of population in the Kurumbarpallam settlement out of 222, the male population is 106 and 116 female population in 53 house holds.

Education

The level of literacy in the settlement for both male and female is very low in the past few generations, because of the factors like ignorance, backwardness, etc. The importance of education is not revealed by the community. They mostly work in agricultural fields. There are total 72 in the age group 5 to 18, out of which 54 are going to school.

There are 130 people in the age group of 19 to 69 out of which 59 never attend schools. 6 person are dropout from the second standard, 5 persons are third standard dropout, 1 person are fourth standard dropout, 21 are fifth standard dropout, 7 are seventh standard dropout, 13 are eighth standard dropout. 9 people have completed tenth standard and 2 persons completed 12th standard. 2 persons have completed UG. 2 Persons are currently doing UG course.

Balwadi

In Balwadi scheme of ICDS, 30 Students are enrolled in the age group of 2 to 5. 8 pregnant Irula women are benefited by ICDS scheme. One teacher and a cook are appointed in the Balwadi. There are 18 children in the age group of 1 to 4, out of this 15 children are attending Balwadi in Kurumbarpallam village. Mid-day meal is provided to them everyday except on Sundays.

Source of drinking water

Piped water is connected near to the household in addition to other sources like streams. The drinking water used by these people is mainly from natural streams. There is hardly any treatment for collected water at home except having it filtered by a cloth. Drinking facilities provided by government especially piped water bore wells are not maintained regularly. In the summer bore wells go dry due to non availability of water. During the dry season, fetching water from streams is the responsibility of women in the households. Most of the time is spent by women collecting water due to shortage of water.

Sanitary Arrangements

In this settlement no house is having latrine. Open defecation is mostly practiced by this community. Four houses sanctioned under the scheme of Pasumai Veedu Thitam with provision of toilet.

Electricity

The houses are powered by the free electricity provided to these settlements which was limited to the usage for just one bulb. But they are using more than one bulb. Electric bill is payable for usage of other electrical appliances. The Irula tribe in this area woke up to the need of electricity when the then ruling government distributed color televisions as a part of fulfilling their election promises as per the manifesto, making them to wonder about the need of television without electricity after which they formally requested the government and got sanctioned.

Possession of Patta for Homestead land

The housing amenities provided to them goes back to the year 1961 which was sanctioned to them by the then CM Mr. Kamarajar. The houses have two rooms which they divide as a kitchen and a hall. There are no lavatory facilities of any kind, which clearly terms this as a poor infrastructure and inadequate housing. The houses are damaged and not maintained properly. Out of 70 households, only 12 houses have patta and 41 are not having patta for their houses. Remaining 17 households live in others houses. Currently under the scheme of Pasumai Veedu thittam , four houses have been sanctioned and the construction is in progress.

Agriculture

The people over there don't have a land confined to them which forces them to cultivate and harvest in a land which is under Forest Department now. Because of which they are also restricted from availing loans from banks and cooperative societies. If the monsoon favors, they cultivate thinai, ragi, maizes, and vegetables like onions, tomatoes, brinjals, peppers, pulses, etc. Prior to the harvest season, animals like boars and elephants enter the cultivated lands and destroy the crops and only a part left for the people. They don't have irrigation facilities and depend upon rain water and natural streams.

Occupation and income

In this settlement, 120 members contribute to the family income. The primary source of income coming through these ways;

Agricultural workers: 11

Animal husbandry: 5

House-keeping in Resorts: 8

Old Age Pension: 3

Petty shop: 1

Wage labor in guest house: 86

The occupation among irula is predominantly wage labors, work in guest houses, some of them engaged in agricultural and allied activities. Recently there is change from there agricultural activities to work as House-keeping person in guest house. The minimum wage for men is Rs.250 and Rs.150 for women in this job. Monthly income of a family is below Rs.5000. Some of them are selling cow milk and cow dung. They get 60 to 70 rupees per basket for cow dung. Cow dung is sold thrice a month.

Communication

Due to lack of transport facilities these people are finding difficulties to go out for their day-to-day work. From public transport system only one mini bus is provided by HADP. Scheduled trips of the bus are 9.00 am, 11.00 am, 5.00 pm and 6.00 pm every day. Jeep is another mode of transport with 15 persons per trip but they need to wait for a long time to get 15 persons for a trip. Hiring a Jeep is very expensive if it is less than 15 persons. There are no good interconnecting roads, ready availability of vehicles for transport from home to health centres. This is a major reason for number of deaths among hill and forest dwellers. Free television provided by the Government and they connected through DTH. Around 70 percent family has mobile connections.

Health

The only access to health care by this settlement is a Primary Health Centre at Masinagudi village. The traveling distance from the tribal settlements to PHC is 7 kilometers. Mobile Health van comes monthly once. Another Mobile Health Unit is provided by a private NGO NAWA (Nilgris Adivasi Welfare Association). Doctor and other Staffs in PHC are not available most of the time. It is very risk to transport the patient if there is emergency at the night because of the wild animals. There is one tribal hospital by ASWINI (Association for Health Welfare in the Nilgiris) at Gudalur. The entire health programme is run and managed by trained tribal youth, consisting of health animators, nurses, lab technician, pharmacists and admin support staff.

Beneficiaries of government plan

Among 53 households four house have sanctioned under pasumai veedu thitam. Free loan provided for buying cow to 5 people. One person benefited loan against petty shop. 4 elder people are getting an old age pension The developmental activities are restricted by forest department due to the place comes under elephant corridor area. Electric fencing is removed by the forest departments in the agricultural fields. Iruals are subjugated by the

Badgas as they are the landlords. Most of the decisions taken for developmental activities are discussed with them for implementation. Even the ward member from irula, she don't have the power to raise voice for their own people. The people suffer as the benefits provided by the government aren't accessible as they have to bribe the officials. The panchayat office is very far from the settlement and a whole day is wasted if they have to visit the panchayat office. Awareness is very less about the developmental programs .Grama panchayat is not functioning properly. MNREGA scheme is also not implemented due to the town panchayat.

Conclusion

Due to landlessness and non availability of irrigation facilities it leads a way of vulnerability. The livelihood of this community is suffered lot in the manner of not providing loan for cultivation in agricultural fields. Grazing animals and collecting Non- timber forest products are restricted by forest department. Wages are very low for both male and female. Most of the earned money is spent for alcohol consumption. In education there is a little bit improvement for attending schools. The quality of drinking water through piped line doesn't carry any purification process. There are no sanitary arrangements provided to this community except the new four houses. The need of transport facilities is not fulfilled. There is only one primary health centre for all their medical treatments. It will be in a limited time.

Post independence the central and state government has initiated many developmental activities to improve the socio economic conditions of tribe yet still there is lack of awareness. Bribe, and political intervention, domination all are show way to became marginalised. Collecting fuel, fodder and minor forest products are restricted due to the poor implementation of the FRA act.

It is also true in context of the land and, unfortunately there are many instances where the local communal resource has been converted to a privately owned commercial resource. Due to the poor awareness, the role of participation in the developmental activities is very minimal. A legal framework is needed for land and access to communal resources.

References

Bakker, L., & Nooteboom, G. (2017). ScienceDirect Anthropology and inclusive development. Current Opinion in Environmental Sustainability, 24, 63–67.

IWGIA – THE INDIGENOUS WORLD – 2016

Padmanabhan, V. K. (2016). Indian Political Science Association, 47(4), 457–472.

TamilNadu Social development report 2008.

Paiement, J. (2007). Anthropology and Development. NAPA Bulletin, 27, 196–223.

Turin.M (2000) Book reviews. (2008) Journal of the Royal Anthropological Institute (N.S.) 14, 890-935.

William L. Partridge, Training manual in development anthropology, American Anthropological Association, 01-Nov-1984.

Chapter - 5

Exploring Cultural Ecology in North East India: A Study among the Tai-Khamti of Arunachal Pradesh

Heerock Jyoti Baruah

In course of evolution, culture has been operating as an essential mechanism for satisfying human needs. In any human society, the concept of need has been understood from two distinct dimensions. White (1943) mentioned about those needs which can be derived out of the resources from within the community and the other consisting of such needs which can be satisfied by depending on the resources of the external world. Human society is naturally connected to its surrounding environment. Human beings, the most creative organism, have long been exploiting the natural resources available in their habitat for the purpose of sustenance and perpetuating their kind. As such, culture has evolved in symbiosis with the physical environment and an alteration in the later often induces a change in the cultural structure of the society dependent on it.

Among, the various sources of the physical environment, forest forms an integral resource base that plays an important role in enhancing the requirement of any society. In the Indian subcontinent, over 53 million tribal people, about 60% of the rural communities directly rely on the forest for their day-to-day requirement (Saha & Sengupta 2014). The North-Eastern states of India host approximately a fourth of the country's forest and as such a large section of its population earn their livelihood from forest-related work. Despite being a renewable natural resource, forest cover has degraded rapidly owing to growing human activities. The National Forest Commission report indicated that around 41% of total forest in India is already degraded, 70% of the forests have no natural regeneration, and

55% of the forests are prone to fire (Banerjee & Chowdhury 2013). A loss of 367 Km^2 of forest cover has been reported between 2009 and 2011 (ibid.).

Various assessments have related this degradation either to population growth, commercial resource extraction and in general economic growth of a region. Apart from these, livelihood concerns of the people living in and around forest areas equally contribute to deforestation. The loss of forest resource induces a reciprocal impact on the forest-dependent communities and their culture. Such stressors may vary between habitat loss, resource crisis, and further social and economic hindrances. In order to cope up with the changing ecological setup, communities take actions either long term or short term and such effort to adapt creates a constant interplay between cultural practices and the environment.

The study of specific influences exerted by the physical environment on human society is quite essential for the interpretation of any culture in terms of its surrounding environment. Following the theoretical formulations of Leslie White, regarding cultural evolution and human adaptation, this research has been targeted to understand the continuity and change of the cultural elements of the Tai-Khamti society, based on their nature and extent of resource utilization (energy) and modes of production (technology).

Study Area

The study is a part of my Ph.D. work, which is being conducted among the Tai Khamti tribe, which is one of the major tribes of the State, distributed in the district of Namsai (earlier Lohit) with a population of 12890 individuals. The Tai Khamti are followers of Theravada Buddhism and

Map 1: District Map of Arunachal Pradesh

Source:MapsofIndia.com

belong to the great Shan race, which migrated to Assam only in the second half of the 18th century from Bor-Khamti near the sources of Irrawady. The first batch of the Khamti which left Bor-Khamti in Upper Burma made their settlement on the Tengapani River located in Namsai district. Since their immigration into India, the Tai-Khamtis have been living in coherence with their ecology. The Lohit frontier has a geographical area of 11402 Km^2 of which 68.36 % is covered by forest.

The strategic location of the Tai Khamti habitat within the forested landscape enhanced their dependency on the resources available in the vicinity. Though the tribe has been practicing settled cultivation, yet during the period from 1948-1996, a tremendous change in the economic activities led to a complete transformation of culture structure for the tribe. The introduction of timber based industries led to the addition and modifications of the traditional cultural elements, which was largely stimulated by the growing urge to make life more secure and attain better standards of living.

Though not deliberately set to improve their culture, the emerging motives of the Tai Khamti tribe during the periods of flourishing timber economy, led to a gradual transformation on the amount of resource harnessed and initiated adjustment onto the modes of production. Thus forest resource has customarily played a critical role in the cultural evolution of the Tai Khamti tribe. Considering this economic dependency and the impact of forest in the socio-cultural life of the tribe, this region has been selected to understand the role of forest resource (energy) in culture building.

Objectives

The prime objectives of the present study are as follows:

- To understand the role of the physical environment on the dynamics of the cultural elements of the Tai Khamti tribe.
- To understand the pattern of strategies adopted by the Tai Khamti to adapt to the changing ecology.

Methodology

The study relied on both qualitative and quantitative data. For the collection of secondary data, sources like journal articles, census reports, newspapers, governmental annual reports, and local manuscripts were analyzed. A major section of the data has been collected through intensive fieldwork in various Tai Khamti habitats, located within the Namsai and Chowkham circle. In course of field work, case studies, life histories, semi-structured interviews, and group discussions were conducted. At the initial stage of the study, a census survey was conducted in the *Kherem* and *Chowkham* village, which helped in identifying informants that were later used for sampling survey. The direct open-ended questionnaire was used to seek a response on the pattern of resource use, the growth of timber trade in the region and understand the traditional rights over the forest landscape and methods of conservation. In order to understand the past scenario of the tribe, interviews were conducted between two groups of informants, one consisting of the elderly members of the tribe (age between 50-60 years and above) and the other comprised of members belonging to the younger generation (age below 50 years). Field observation and photographs were much helpful to acquire on-site data relating to the prevalent timbering activities, reformed agricultural practices and other livelihood opportunities generated in the post-bàn period. Throughout the study, snowball sampling has been much helpful.

Results and Discussion

A long history of habitation in the forested landscape of the Lohit frontier of Arunachal Pradesh has equipped the Tai Khamti community with a rich knowledge about their ecology, which has helped them to efficiently harness the resources available, based on their socio-cultural and economic needs. The important elements of such accumulated knowledge are portrayed in their innovation in medicine making, food habits, the pattern of construction, means of acquiring a livelihood, traditional healing practices and in their skills pertaining to fishing and hunting. The prime purpose of this research paper being an examination of the continuity and change of the cultural elements of the Tai Khamti tribe, the following paragraph will begin with a discussion on the nature-culture symbiosis.

Forest and Tai Khamti

The Tai Khamti socio-cultural life is closely attached to their surrounding landscape. The symbiotic relationship with the physical environment can be observed from their established socio-religious and cultural practices. The Khamtis derives a large portion of their daily needs from the resources available in their vicinity. A part of their daily life is devoted to the collection of non-timber forest produce, which includes roots, tubers, leaves and other wild varieties of eatables and construction materials like bamboo, cane, etc. The forest resource contributes to their demand for fuelwood and animal fodder. A traditional system of medicine making and healing practice has been well associated with the Khamti culture. This age-old tradition derives its essential requirements from the varieties of medicinal plants found in the region (Table 1).

Though Tai Khamti has been a strong believer of Theravada Buddhism, yet they simultaneously practice worshiping of the spirits of the forests. This tradition exerts an authority that directs villagers to seek the permission of the spirit of the Manabhum Hills or the *Dangoria* before any attempt to procure the forest resources. Such ceremony is even solemnized in case of crop failure and even in a situation where the whole village seeks blessings if subjected to unseen misfortune. The easy availability of raw materials has encouraged a flourishing handicraft economy among the tribe. Craftwork on bamboo, cane, wood, and ivory have been significant among the tribe (Fig 1). Most common among these were wooden Buddha statue, bamboo basket, cane furniture, weapons, etc. Their finest artworks can still be noticed during the *Poong* celebration, which is a Tai Khamti drama, wherein each of the characters has to dress in a unique costume which is self-made within the community.

Table 1: Medicinal plants used by the Tai Khamti

Medicinal Plants	*Scientific Name*	*Parts Used*
King Pang	Alpina Yalanga Willd	Leaves
Tora	Alpina Malaccensis	Leaves
Simul	Bombak Ceiba	Bark
Manimuni	Centella Asciatica	Leaves
Medicinal Plants	Scientific Name	Parts Used
Dubori	Cynodon dactylon	Grass
Sepak	Euphorbia Neriifolia	Leaves
Key Bon	Cyperus brevifolius	Grass
Leta Gosh	Caesalpinia Bonduc	Seed
Lefafu	Clerodendrum Colebrookianum	Leaves
Meteka	Millingtonia Hortensis	Leaves
Nol Khagori	Phragmites Karka	Grass
Outenga	Dillenia Indica	Fruit
Pipli	Piper mullesua	Seed and leaves
Yahangeng	Stachytarpheta Cayennensis	Leaves
Hilikha	Terminalia Bellirical	Seed

Tai Khamti is known for their mastery over catching and rearing of elephants. This tradition has been carried along by the tribe in course of their migration from Burma. The dense forest landscape of the Lohit Frontier and the locational advantage of the Khamti habitat provided them a platform to continue the tradition of elephant rearing. The wide distribution of elephants in the Roing reserve and an ample supply of fodder helped the tribe maintain the consistency of the tradition across history. This distinctive capability has been a vital reason for the rapid expansion of timber trade in the region. Though the commercial extraction of forest resource in the Tai Khamti territory dates back to the British era, yet the post-independence period was characterized by the tremendous growth of timber operation from within the community. The role of Tai Khamti elites has been significant in the establishment of sawmills and in harnessing a new source of energy for livelihood generation.

Fig 1: Tai-Khamti Craftsman along with his Bamboo and Cane Crafts

Resource Harnessed and Cultural Development

In the preceding paragraph, it has been established that different cultural elements of the Tai Khamti draw direct impetus from the ecological setting. The pattern of resource use prevalent among the tribes was largely stimulated by their personal and societal needs. Like other forest fringe community, the Tai Khamti has been exploiting the resources of their habitat in some way or the other to sustain their life and maintain the stability of the society. Since their migration into India in the 18th century, the Tai Khamti has been practicing settled cultivation. Paddy is the main crop grown, which forms their staple food. They have historically been cultivating *lahi* as the main variety of paddy. Given the sandy nature of the landscape and lack of sufficient technology to enhance agricultural productivity, the output was limited with a minimal surplus. The earliest Tai Khamti society has largely been structured around their agricultural economy and many of the cultural elements showed cohesion with the agricultural activities. For example, the society was characterized by strong cohesive bond among the members and prevalence of joint family system which were essential requite for performing the agricultural works. Due to the lack of surplus, trade was limited and occasionally exchange of goods was carried out at Dhola in lieu of paddy. Though the Khamtis are referred to as an advanced tribe of North-east India, owing to their literary capabilities and possession of own script, yet the growth of their culture remained quite static due to i) the lack of better source to harness more quantities of energy in comparison to agriculture and ii) the lack of efficiency of the mechanism used to expend the already harnessed energy (agriculture).

Table 2: Timber Industries Operating in Lohit District till 1996

Name	***Place***
Arunachal Plywood Industries Limited	Namsai
Mein Wood Industry	Chowkham
Tafragam Vineer Mill	Tafragam
Tumba Saw Mill	Wakro
Chaukham Saw Mill	Chowkham
Tafragam Saw Mill	Tafragam
Name	Place
Arunachal Wood Industry	Tafragam
M.K Timber	Tezu
Namchoom Saw Mill	Tezu
Kamlang Saw Mill	Wakro
Lohit Saw Mill and Vineer Mill	Sunpura
Lavto Saw Mill	Medo
Mantau Saw Mill	Chowkham
Bijoyshree Wood Industry	Namsai
Eastern saw Mill	Chowkham
Namsai Timber	Namsai

Source: *Field Questionnaire Survey*

In the context of the Tai Khamti tribe, the human-energy stage of the cultural development progress was achieved with the emergence of the timber economy in the region. The timber trade, as a new and better source of energy generation, bore significant potential to fuel the progress of the community across the ladder of cultural development. With the first timber mill set up at Sunpura in 1948, the tribe increased their capacity to harness forest resource and put it to a better income generating sector. The increase in energy flow was supported by improvement in the technology used to expend the resource. For example, trucks were widely owned across the Khamti households to enhance the timber procuring ability. The region simultaneously experienced a significant inflow of manpower from the neighboring State of Assam and as such, the access to better energy source supplemented by mechanical efficiency led to a significant rise in the number of sawmills in the region.

There is no denying the fact that, the timber economy did bring significant development to the Tai Khamti tribe. The material gains significantly increased in comparison to the agricultural economy. The growth of economic wealth helped the tribe to secure noteworthy status in the political and cultural affairs. In course of the study it was found that, during the flourishing timber economy, there has been a prevailing tendency among the youths to study outside the state which consequently led to cultural assimilation among the tribe. According to the informants, during the period from 1950 to 1996, every Tai Khamti household had at least one individual involved in the trade. The widespread resource exploitation led to the recognition of Chowkham, a Tai Khamti village, as the richest village of Asia. The new energy source (timber) harnessed by the tribe was more lucrative mode for livelihood generation and the profits generated was much higher compared to the agricultural activities. The emergence of timber trade provided the community with better opportunities to secure their sustenance achieve higher living standards and increase production for exchange and sale. However, the cultural progression that emerged out of the new economy equally conflicted with the old social system. The accumulation of wealth and increased competition in trade significantly reduced social cohesion. Disengagement from agricultural activities loosened the joint family system in due course. Marriage rules have been slackened with the growing assimilation which paved the way to inter-tribe marriage, which was strictly regulated among the tribe. Many of the informants also associated the increase in money flow from the timber trade to the growing case of consumption of intoxicants within the community.

Cultural Recession and Ecological Adaptation

So far we have learned that the physical environment significantly influence the cultural traits of the Tai Khamti tribe and in their effort to harness additional quantities of energy by tapping new sources (from agriculture to timber economy), the tribe had initiated a process of addition and modification of their traditional cultural elements. However, this advancement of culture was not continuous and without limit. In the year 1996, following a petition filed by T.N Godavarman, the Supreme Court of India placed a complete ban of timber trade to check deforestation in the whole country. This judgment jeopardized the timber economy of the North-Eastern region and placed a ban on the transportation of timber from the region.

The ban on timber has not only affected the mill owners and contractors but also the tribe as a whole, as the forest resource had by then became the primary source of subsistence. The sudden ban on the trade came as a shock for the tribe as the timber industry represented the largest employment sector in the region. Larger social issues emerged in the post-ban period that included an increase in school dropout due to the instability of family economic condition. Disengagement from agricultural activities during the period of timber operation and lack of savings owing to the easy means of livelihood led a section of the tribe towards depression and eventually stimulated them to engage in the consumption of opium. The lack of sufficient savings, made it difficult for the economically marginalized families, either to cope up with the situation or invest in other means of livelihood. Such efforts were restricted only to the Tai Khamti elites, who they started investing in other economic sectors like tea plantations, tea industry, schools, brick industries, etc. Such inequalities in income generation marked the growth of class hierarchy and gradually loosened the social support system within the community.

In the context of the Tai Khamti, the timber ban has been the leading factor that limited the capacity of the tribe to expand the energy harnessed and in the absence of a greater magnitude of energy source; the society experienced a cultural recession in the post timer ban period. White (1943) states, "If we can continue to harness as much energy per capita per year in the future as we are doing now, there is little doubt but that our old social system will give way to a new one, a new era of civilization. Should, however, the amount of energy that we are able to harness diminish materially, then culture would cease to advance or even recede".

Though the ban on timber restricted the economic development of the Tai Khamti tribe for nearly a decade, yet a gradual process of adaptation through securing their means of livelihood can be observed in their present-day society. Among the structural changes introduced by the Tai Khamti tribe to cope up in the post-ban period, the transformation in their agricultural pattern needs special mention (Fig 2). The traditional agricultural practices of the Tai Khamti have been specific towards the cultivation of paddy, largely for the purpose of consumption with a limited approach towards trading the surplus. The growing dominance of timber-based income avenues created a significant shift of occupation from 1970 to 1990 and this gradually restricted the agricultural activities to means of subsistence rather than generating income. However, this scenario has undergone vital change over the decade. In course of the study, it was revealed that out of fifty former timber traders interviewed, 60% have shifted to agriculture. A strict line of distinction can be easily drawn between their traditional system of cultivation and the more formalized means adopted in the present day.

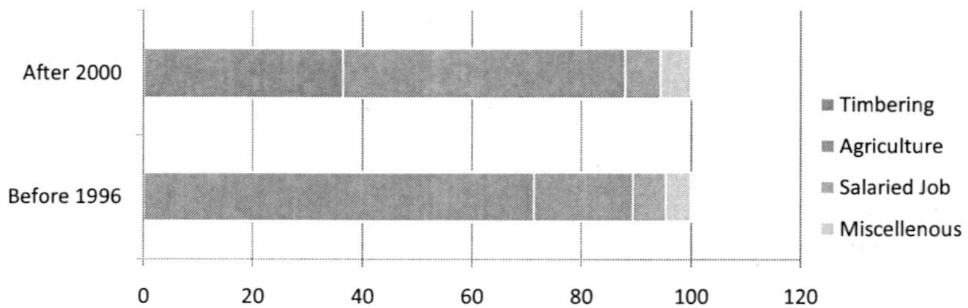

Source: *Field sample survey*

Fig 2: Occupational Shift in Kherem Village in the Post-Ban Period

In course of the study, a gradual change of perception towards utilization of agricultural technology has been observed among the tribe. In the Kherem village, which comprises of fifty-one households, sixteen families were identified who owned modern farming equipment including, tractors, cultivator, chisel plow and harrow, while one of the households reported having backhoe loader for agricultural activities.

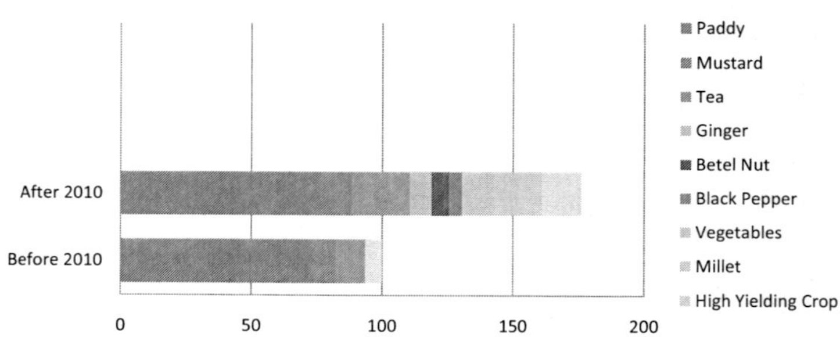

Source: *Field Sample Survey*

Fig 3: Crop Distribution Pattern in Kherem and Chowkham Village

The agricultural transformation observed in the Tai Khamti territory has been largely the byproduct of their efforts of adaptation against the economic stagnation arising out of the timber ban of 1996. In spite of the extension of agricultural activities, the present Tai Khamti society portrays a slow cultural progress owing to the fact that, the energy gained from the expansion of agricultural activities has not attained the level of growth that can substitute what was derived from the timber trade. Thus it is a prime necessity at this time that the governments looks into the ecological stresses and provide them access to new avenues of survival opportunities.

Conclusion

Timber based economy tremendously increased the amount of resource harnessed by the Khamtis and as a consequence, a sequential growth of culture was experienced. With the maturation of the timber procuring equipment and increase in the flow of manpower into the timber trade, there has been acceleration in the capacity to exploit resources, the growth of living standards and advancement in political sectors. The Tai Khamti after their long-term dependency on agriculture and non-timber forest resources gradually shifted towards the lucrative timber business. Though no deliberately aimed towards the development of their culture, this shift in the modes of securing livelihoods and transformation in the utilization of the physical environment, in due course increased the portion of individuals separating from agriculture. The accumulation of wealth and competition resulted in the formation of smaller grouping within the society and thus loosened the social capital. At the beginning of the shift, the tribe was extremely inclined towards harnessing the maximum amount of energy possible in the form of timber, which opened scope for a large accumulation of wealth. With the sequence of industrial growth, the energy per capita has considerably increased among the Tai Khamti and the stage of cultural development was achieved through superior literary advancement, increased political autonomy, organized social structure and access to better technology. Thus the Tai Khamti society would never have advanced substantially beyond the levels already reached in the agricultural economy, unless the efforts to harness the greater magnitude of energy through the timber were not introduced.

In the post-timber ban period, the tribe had experienced a stage of cultural recession following the restrictions imposed on the flow of energy that has been previously utilized for culture-building. The finite and limited access to timber trade created irregularities in income distribution leading to a more pronounced class hierarchy within the society. Disengagement from agriculture and lack of savings made it difficult for people to invest in other means of production. The lack of adequate opportunities to harness additional energy from new sources significantly contributed to the declining social fabrics of the Tai Khamti tribe. The widespread of opium consumption among the Khamtis following the loss of livelihood sources emerged as a new threat that alienated much of its population from social contact and created stagnation in socio-economic activities within the society.

In an attempt to cope up with the cultural recession originating from the degradation of resource flow, the Tai Khamti have gradually started to exploit the easiest available environmental resource in their surrounding, which is the land resource. The Tai Khamti dominated territory has been characterized by large tract of unused land as compared to the scanty population. In any human society, adaptation strategies are derived from the nature of resource available in a given habitat. These days, the Tai Khamti have revived their traditional agricultural patterns to survive the changing ecological conditions. Introductions of crop variety, expansion of cropland, the practice of multiple cropping, use of modern equipment to enhance production forms an effort to substitute the energy derived from the timber trade, which has turned out to be less profitable these days. A significant shift of occupation from timber business to agricultural activities has become prominent among the tribe. The Tai Khamti society has portrayed a slow cultural progress in the post timber ban period owing to the fact that, the energy gained from the expansion of agricultural activities has not attained the level of growth that can substitute what was derived from the timber trade. In the present context, the cultural development of the Tai Khamti tribe largely depends on their ability to challenge the ecological constraints, either by means of harnessing a new source of energy or by expanding the efficiency of the technological means which are currently being utilized for putting the available resources to use. Thus enhancing the ability to exploit the physical environment and gaining maximum benefits from the challenging ecology might turn out to be beneficial for the Tai Khamti tribe in the near future.

References

Albrecht, D. E, and Murdock, S.H. "Natural Resource Availability and Social Change". *Sociological Enquiry,* vol. 3, no. 56, 1986, pp. 381–395.

Banerjee, A, and Chowdhury, M. "Forest Degradation and Livelihood of Local Communities in India: A Human Rights Approach". *Journal of Horticulture and Forestry,* vol. 5, no. 8, 2013, pp. 122–129.

Bennett, J. W. "The Interaction of Culture and Environment in the Smaller Societies." *American Anthropologist*, vol. 46, no. 4, 1944, pp. 461–478.

Chakravarty, S, et al. "Deforestation: Causes, Effects and Control Strategies." *Global Perspectives on Sustainable Forest Management*, 2012, pp. 3–28.

Dangwal, D.D. *Commercialisation of Forests, Timber Extraction and Deforestation in Uttaranchal, 1815-1947*. 6 Aug. 2018, www.conservationandsociety.org .

Descola , P, and Pailsson, G . *Nature and Society: Anthropological Perspectives*. Routledge, 2004.

Edgerton, R. B. "Cultural vs Ecological Factors in the Expression of Values, Attitudes, and Personality Characteristics." *American Anthropologist*, vol. 67, no. 2, 1965, pp. 442–446.

Engelman, et al. "Population as a Scale Factors: Impacts on Environment and Development." *Population, Environment, and Development*, Tata Energy Research Institute, 1997, pp. 15–33.

Freilich, M. "Ecology and Culture: Environmental Determinism and the Ecological Approach in Anthropology." *Anthropological Quarterly*, vol. 40, no. 1, 1967, pp. 26–43.

Gogoi , Lila. *The Tai Khamtis*. Chowkhamoon Gohain (Namsoom), Chowkham: NEFA, 1971.

Haenn, N, and Wilk, R. R. *The Environment in Anthropology: A Reader in Ecology, Culture, and Sustainable Living*. New York University Press, New York, 2006.

Laine, Nicholas. "Effects of the 1996 Timber Ban in Northeast India: The Case of the Khamtis of Lohit District, Arunachal Pradesh."*Nature, Environment and Society: Conservation, Governance and Transformation in India*, Orient Blackswan, 2012, pp. 73–93.

Meggers, B. J. "Environmental Limitation on the Development of Culture." *American Anthropologist*, vol. 56, no. 5, 1954, pp. 801–824.

Messerschmidt, D. A. "Ecological Change and Adaptation among the Gurungs of the Nepal Himalaya." *Human Ecology*, vol. 4, no. 2, 1976, pp. 167–185.

Moran, E. F. *People and Nature: An Introduction to Human Ecological Relations*. Blackwell Publishing, USA, 2006.

Nayak, B.P, et al. *Livelihood of Local Communities and Forest Degradation in India: Issues for REDD* . Ministry of Environment and Forests, Government of India, 15 Sept. 2018, www.moef.nic.in/sites/default/files/redd-bk3.pdf.

Oliver, S. C. *Ecology and Cultural Continuity as Contributing Factors in the Social Organization of the Plains Indians*. University of California Press, Berkeley, 1962.

O'Neil, Dr. D. *Culture Change: An Introduction to the Processes and Consequences of Culture Change*. California, 1997.

Saha, M, and Sengupta, S. "Symbiotic Relationship between Forest and Tribe: A Case Study of Santal Tribe of Jaypur Forest, Bankura District, West Bengal, India." *Transactions,* vol. 36, no. 2, 2014, pp. 235-246.

Sarma, M, and Choudhury, B. "Continuity and Change of Certain Culturally Coded Survival Strategies of the Misings of Brahmaputra River Valley of Assam." *Journal of Human Ecology*, vol. 49, no. 2, 2015, pp. 129–137.

Sarkar, J. *Society, Culture, and Ecological Adaptation among Three Tribes of Arunachal Pradesh*. Anthropological Survey of India, Kolkata, Ministry of Human Resource Development, Dept. of Culture, Govt. of India, 1987.

Upadhyay, S, et al. *India's Forests and the Judiciary: The Godavarman Story*. World Wide Fund for Nature, New Delhi, 2009.

Verma, J, and Kirpal, B. "T.N. Godavarman Thirumulkpad vs Union Of India & Ors on 12 December, 1996 ." *Indian Kanoon*, indiankanoon.org/doc/298957/.

White, Leslie. A. "Energy and Evolution of Culture". *American Anthropologist*, vol. 45, no. 3, 1943, pp. 335-356.

Chapter - 6

Current Social Changing Scenario in Musahar Scheduled Caste of Bihar

Jokhan Sharma

Social change is the process of the alteration with more references of quality of change. Social Change of society is related to change in culture, co-resistance, and growth of modern technology as part of the culture has been closely associated with alteration in the economic structure on important part of the society (Khare, 1984). In social science, term 'Social change' refers to alteration in non-material culture that is occurring in the social structure and social relationship of a social group or society. It may occur in norms, values, cultural products and symbol in society (Dumont, 1970; Beteille, 1996). The alteration in the structure in functional social system, institution and patterns of interaction, work, leaser activities work and other aspect of the society can be altered over the time as a result of the process of the change (Rogers, 1962; Boskoff, 1972). Such changes are believed to often follow other innovations including the technological ones. Economic, social, political, religious factors etc generate alterations and hence change. The active process of alteration work may include acculturation, diffusion, assimilation, transculturation etc. (Mann, 1987; Sen, 2008).

Social change are wide and numerous. The interpretation of social change is task beset by great difficulties. So many sociologists and anthropologists express their own view on 'social change' (Aiyappan, 1994; Dube, 1958; Malinowski, 1958; Sahu, 2009 Mann, 1987 etc). Green, Arnold (1960) says that "*social change occurs because all societies are in a constant state of disequilibrium*". It means the state of disequilibrium marking societies. Maclver and Page (1959) argued that '*social change is a process responsive to many types of changes, to changes in the man-made conditions of living , to changes in the attitudes and beliefs of man, and to changes that go back beyond human control, to the biological and physical nature of things'*. M. N. Srinivas (1962, 1966 & 1977) argues that "the crux of social change phenomenon the actual process of social change is one of dynamic, the several factors acting and reacting upon each other, so that, in the final result, it would the dependent variables."

Social change is its 'Haphazard' nature on the one hand and 'intended' or 'purposed' on the other hand. In India context, the massive programmes of planned changed in society have been framed and implemented. The basic idea is to develop these underdeveloped or maganalised societies within certain specific aims and objectives.

The Indian scheduled caste communities have been characterized with complex social system and sub systems. The linguistic, ethnic, racial, religious, social and cultural diversities have always enthused and perpetuated their respective kind. With such complex social framework of rural India, the various element of purposed change, over the years, have reacted in certain definite way and could develop definite equation with the ongoing ingredients of Indian rural social structure (Dube, 1958; Singh, 1980; Ahuja, 2011). These can be explained through compatibility, incompatibility, acceptance, rejection, opposition, indifference, success, failure etc.

The social scientist, their knowledge and research also claimed for their usefulness in the creation and gearing up of change among the marginalized or backward communities (Srinivas, 1958; Thorat, 2002). But what has been their real contribution, in the context of helping induction of planned change in these communities in our country, has not been, at macro-level, explained. It is done only at conceptual level that they asserted or they really practically helped bringing about change by identifying areas of strange and weakness inherent in Indian rural social systems. Some scholars have tried to analyze the change in the status, attitude and aspirations of scheduled castes with reference to social development and economic change on the Indian scene since the days we attained Independence. It has been brought out by these scholars that there is a wind of change and some improvement may be seen in respect of thrust on social mobility of scheduled castes at different levels like, individual, family and corporate. Brief conclusions of some of these scholars in brief account.

In 1946, Ambedkar wrote a commendable book '*Who were the Sudras*' in which he has defined the Sudras and highlighted their deplorable condition. In other book *'The Untouchables' (1948)* he has described the lower status and poor socio-economic condition of the scheduled castes. He is the first man to use the political name to change the condition of status of the scheduled castes. He considered political power a necessity for the political salvation of Scheduled castes.

In Book '*Inside Bihar (1956)*' P.C. Roy Chaudhary depicts the intercaste relations of the scheduled caste. Besides the Chamars, the Doms, the Dhobis, the Dusadhs, the Bhuiyas, The Pasis, the Hari, he has written on Mushars as well.

Andre Beteille (1966) in his book '*Caste, Class and Power*' gives the details of relation between the Brahmin, the non- Brahmin and the Untouchable castes of *Praiya* and *Palla*. Adoption of certain Sanskritization practices and education enable the untouchables to compete with the Brahmins on the equal terms for jobs. They find that because of Sanskritization, the scheduled caste have not changed their occupation but they have given up taking forbidden items of food and are also discouraging widow marriage.

Sachchidanand in '*The Harijan Elite*' (1976) find that among Harijans education, reservation of post and grant of other privileges have created a new middle class. The men of lower *shastra* have thus a better chance to achieve high economic and political status. This study reveals the status of the 'Harijan Educated Elite' in their own society and in the other wider local communities.

There are many study have find that the status of Scheduled Caste is in a process of transition (Vidyarthi, 1977; Khare, 1984; Beteile, 1996, Nayak, 2012, Sharma, 2015). Legal and constitutional measures may not have brought about a perceptible change in their status but it is in the process of change and in times to some it is mostly to bring about a change in the attitude structure of scheduled caste peoples.

After post independent, massive pragrammes, projects and schemes of rural development has been initiated by Government to bring about desired change among Indian rural communities, specially including the scheduled caste and scheduled tribe (Singh, 2014, Ahuja, 2011, Patnaik, 201, Sahu, 2009, Sharma, 2012, Nayak, 2012). The overall purview of Five Year Plans, were started to provide impetus to development and change in village India. This accelerated the Process of change and consequently social dynamic. In certain communities and in certain areas and spheres the planned change has been more effective than others. But in other spheres and areas the changes efforts failed to achieve the intended purpose. The response remained partial in yet other aspects. Plurality and heterogeneity of village India, with its diverse social cultural systems and sub-systems, have had their own say in the matter (Lynch, 1969).

Intimately connected with constitutional safeguards that have an important bearing on the upliftment of SCs there is still another provision in the Constitution for reservation of seats both houses of the Parliament and states Assemblies, of job both in the public and private sectors, of seats in educational institution and many other spheres. Mention may here be made of the provision contained in Article 16(4), 46,330, 332, 335, 338, 339 and 340. Although the government never explicitly said that these provisions are being incorporated in the Constitution with a view to eliminate or to reduce the alienation of SCs, it may be safely inferred that at least the intention of the government was as such. Probably, the policy-makers thought that it would not only give SCs a sense of belongingness to the body polity of Indian Society but would also provide room for both non-scheduled and Scheduled caste to interact with each other and to forge a better understanding between them. When both these group would learn to live together, the various stereotypes and prejudices relating to the SCs would gradually disappear and that it would further offer them an opportunities to improve their social, economic and ritual status without any fear or humiliation.

Philosophy of This Study

The problems of the Scheduled Castes in India have receives scarce attention of the sociologists and Anthropologists. Most of Scheduled caste studies are done as a political, philosophical and literaturally point of views (Srinivas, 1958; Ghurye, 1969, Beteille, 1996; Lynch, 1969; Khan, 1980; Mukhaerjee, 2002). There are only few anthropological studies in Bihar, Sachchidanada's (1977) "Harijan Elite" and Vidyarthi's & Mishra's (1977) "Harijan Today" are pioneer studies in this field. But no specific study on Musahar Scheduled Caste has been done so far. A review of literature reveals that there are no comprehensive studies of the nature. Studies made by a few scholars touch mostly the subject of untouchability which constitutes one of the most important aspects of the social cultural problems of the Musahar Schedule caste (Prassad, 1988; Sharma, 1998; Thorat, 2002; Sinha, 2005; O'Malley, 2007 & Saday, 2011). On the availability of literature sources some figure comes out on researcher mind is that the Musahar community is still backward and marginalized. They are still found suppressed, exploited, neglected and forced to live insecure life because of illiteracy, ill health, poverty, migration and discriminatory social system.

At present time, with the great change in the fields of education, technology, communication, transport etc and their interaction with different cultural/caste groups, they must have undergone certain changes. Due to these changes affected and empowering to the Musahar community in process of social change. The common objective of the study is to explore the changing way of life of the Musahar community in respective of cultural practices, social life and organizational setup in the study area.

To achieve these research objectives the study will be carried out to Musahar scheduled caste of Rohtas district, Bihar State. The study shall make a significant contribution in social inclusion of Musahar community of India. This qualitative research paper presented is based on the fieldwork. The primary date was collected from fieldwork through observation, formal discussion with peoples and unstructured interview and interview with key informants. The reference were taken from secondary data from various sources like Web sources, census of India Data, District gazetteer, District development office report and publish and unpublished literature through various institutions library etc.

The Musahar Scheduled Caste

Nomenclature and Origin

Oral tradition suggests that they were ancient nomadic and hunting tribes (Lockwood, 1878; Roy, 1935; Nesufiled, 1888; Ghurye, 1969; Blunt, 1969; Crooke,1896). During nomadic life, they ate whatever found in the nature. The word 'Musahar' derived from their Dietary inclination of Mouse (shah and Saday, 2011). It is facts that they used to maintain their living by catching and eating the mouse found in the open field. Sir, Risley Herbert (1891), a colonial official wrote, "Mushar literally mean 'rat-taker or 'rat-eater' (from '*musa*' which mean rat and '*hera*' means' seeker) or even 'flesh-seeker' or 'hunter' ('*musa*' mean flesh). Even the nomenclature the community bears is a stereotype invested with these stigma 'those who eat rats-rat meat being regarded as the sustenance of the untouchable. Ghurye (1969) said that they are the rat-eaters group and they eat rats (*'Musa'* in local language), it is likely that they are known as Musahar.

They claimed that they are the descendants of great sage Valmiki, the author of religious epic The Ramayan. Some Musahars trace their origin to the legend of the low caste women Sabari a devotee of god 'Ram' in the great Hindu epic the Ramayan. By virtue of her love and devotion of Lord Ram who is regarded as in carnation of Lord Vishnu, she came to occupy an exalted position in the galaxy of great devotees (Singh, 1992).

The origin of the Musahars, who are known by different names in Bihar and its adjoining states, has still re-mained debatable. In colonial ethnographic works they have been related to different tribes both within and outside the region based on etymological explanation and anthropometrical indices. While J. C. Nesûfield, 1888, 'The Musahars of Central and Upper India', Calcutta Review, 171: 1–52, linked their origin to the Kol and Cheru tribes of Chotanagpur based on legendary myths of 'Deosi', H. H. Risley's,1891, Tribes and Castes of Bengal, Vol. I & II, Kolkata: Firma KLM, hypothesis based on the etymological explanation of the word Musahar (rat-eater or rat-catcher) traces their origin to the equally Dravidian Bhuiyas of southern Chotanagpur. Meanwhile, Indian ethnologist S. C. Roy, 1935, 'Report of Anthropological Work 1930-31: Hill Bhuinyas of Orissa', Journal of Bihar and Orissa Research Society, xviii: 51–78; and 1935b, 'Report of Anthropological Work in 1932-33: The Bhuinyas and Their Congeners', Journal of Bihar and Orissa Research Society, Past I, xxi: 1–19, links their origin to the independent section of the old 'Desh Bhuiyas' or 'Pauri Bhuiyas' in the tributary state of Orissa. For detail discussions see Gyan Prakash, 1990, Bonded Histories: Genealogies of Labour Servitude in Colonial India, Cambridge: Cambridge University Press. Presently it is in the Magadh region of Bihar where they have the greatest concentration, and are known as 'Bhuinyas' (Sharma, 1998).

The Musahars are one of the most deprived communities in India. Constitutionally they are comes under Scheduled Caste category. In Bihar, they were given Maha-Dalit (lowest among the low) status by the state government in years 2007, testament to the abject penury in which most live. The major scheduled caste groups in this region are Chamar, Dusadh, Musahar, Dom, Pasi etc. Musahar presence in Bihar is significant- they constitute the third largest within the scheduled caste population in the state.

There is belief that part of them entered to this region from Magadh and the others from Tirhut (Mithala) partly in Bihar, India. They are mostly located in Bihar, Uttar Pradesh, Jharkhand and West Bengal. In Bihar State they are concentrated several districts like Rohtas, Gaya, Aara, Bhagalpur, Madhubani, Mazaffarpur, Darbhanga, Champaran etc.

In the 1935 census, Musahars (together with Bhuinya population) were considered as tribes but for the first time in the 1961 census they were put in the Scheduled Caste category. In Bihar, according to the 1981 census, the entire population of the Musahars amounted to 13, 91,000 and that of the Bhuinya as to 8, 50,469. According to this count, the population of the

Musahars and the Bhuinyas taken millionaire castes' in the state of Bihar. Musahars is one of them. According to census 2011, the total population of the Musahars people in India is 2,725,114 (male-1407557 & female-1317557) and across the country are 3,037,000 (Joshua Project). The other two being the '*Chamars*' (3 million) and the '*Dusadhs*' (2.7 million). According to census 2011 their sex ratio is 936 females per thousand male persons.

Social changes among the Musahar Scheduled Caste

Social changes are rapidly coming and in fact their occurrence is inevitable. But what is the rate of social change. A change may occur in different societies or in the same society at different times (Mann, 1987; Srinivas; 1966 & Singh, 1980). It is more or less impossible to decide about the rapidity of change and determine whether change is faster than the other.

To introduce social change in a Musahar community there are two ways- the direct and the indirect (Cohen, 1986 & Goodwin, 2009). The direct way means the implementation of various schemes and programmes meant to bring about changes among Musahar community. Secondly, the indirect way means the protective legislation; this is certain law and enactments to keep the people confined to a situation defined to be responsible factors for the creation of changes of the community. In the Musahar community where changes have taken place in their cultural surroundings, there has been a marked change in their social environment. The Musahar community of the study area, they were considered exploited and backward in earlier periods. But in today, some changes come out in their living condition and livelihood situation.

Life cycle rituals in The Musahar community

Traditionally, there is no special function celebrated during women conceived a child. But they contact with other Hindu caste group they started a symbolic function like *'Chhatti'* ceremony- birth celebration on the sixth day after delivery and another function known as *'Muhjuthi'* ceremony for the first feeding of cereals by baby. These function mainly celebrated on the occasion of Male child birth.

In Musahar community marriage ceremony celebrated according to Hindu Customs and rituals likes *Barachaya* (engagement), *Tikal, Barat, Marwapuja, Haldi puja, Matkor, samdhimilan, gurhathi, kanyadan, sindurdan, bidai, chouthari* etc. Marriage ceremony rituals completed by

Brahmins (Pandit). The service of a 'Nai' is essential and marriage is solemnized in front of the Sacred Fire.

After the death, the body is cremated and mortuary rites include '*Hajamat*' (male relatives get their heads shaved), '*Pinddan*' and '*Saradh*' are performed.

Food Habit

Generally they are non-vegetarian by habit and choice. Their traditions and origin are indicative enough that they eat flesh of all animals, wild as well as domesticated. They eat pork, fowls, ducks, eggs, field rats, rabbits and flesh of dead animals. Their daily food consists of coarse rice (*Bhaat*), bread (*Roti),* vegetables curry (*Tarkaari*) and pulse. Since they can rarely afford to take mutton, fish or goat meat, they usually purchase intestines, head or rejected pieces of meat and cook it. They are addicted to liquor which is locally prepared from '*mahua*' flower or barley. Chewing of tobacco mixed with lime is common habit among them.

When considering the food which the Musahar consume, it is necessary to bear in mind their segregation from the rest of society and the limitations placed upon their opportunities to earn as well as upon their abject poverty.

Social Inclusion at village level

During filed work, the researchers found that today the social interaction between Musahar and non Musahar communities some better condition from the early periods. Social condition of the village has been a change in the attitude of the non-Musahar towards the Musahar communities. Direct evidence of this is the group activities that are organized at the village level, such as village worship, village community meetings, organized fairs and festivals, wedding ceremonies etc. other caste people of the village are also invited them and they participated in such functions.

In many villages, during the worship of the Goddess of the village, the procession (*Shobhayatra*) of the Goddess also passes through *Musahar Tolas*. In such types of religious and social function organized at the village level they contributed financially and physically. Apart from this, their participation can be seen on religious occasions such as Durga Pooja, Holi, Chhath Pooja etc. However, on these occasions, their involvement is limited. But these initial changes in the changing attitudes of the village society towards the Musahar are a good sign. By looking at the changing environment of the village it can be said that discrimination against these backward societies will be reduced in the village and the role of village peoples in the full development of these societies will be important.

Marriage System

This changing process can be seen in the present time also. Presently, some changes to be seen in the context of their marriage practice due to their close contact with Non-Musahar and other societies. Earlier, where the people of their caste play to role of mediator called *'Aguaa'* in marriage proposal, but today this responsibility is also being performed by people of non-Musahar people.

At the same time, the trend of other forms of marriage such as love marriage, marriage by captured, running marriage etc. can be seen in the new generation. However, this type of marriage is limited to their society. These people do not get married in Non-Musahar societies.

The main reason behind such marriages is that new generation people become self-reliant by working in other states in search of employment and earning money there. Due to this self-dependency and autonomy grownup in Musahar youth mentality, they take the decision of their marriage itself. Along with this, they are also influenced by modern culture and society.

Child marriage was a common practice in these societies. But, today the practice has reduced considerably. It has been possible due to the efforts of non-government and government institutions, which led to the awareness of child marriage in this community, and also provided information about the problems that arise as well as its unlawfulness.

Divorce and Remarriage

The concept of divorces among the Musahar is based on customary practices. There is no court involved and a women or man is permitted to leave their spouse in case of differences.

Widow remarriage is an accepted practices among the Mushar community remarriage is considerd only if the widow is still young. Once the age of fecundity has been crossed they do not usually remarry. The local term for widow is '*Kuwar*' and widower is '*Randawa*'. Such females and male are usually reclaimed by the husband's clan through the custom of levirate or by the wife's clan through the custom of sorority, respectively. However, a widow's status in their society is not high and she is debarred from taking part in certain ritual and ceremonial activities.

Religious Belief and Practices among the Musahar

Traditionally they follow their tribal Faith and will worship their family deity, the village as well as the gods of the wider Hindu faith. Musahar people continue to attribute their occurrence to the supernaturals, including supreme god. People take help of supernatural element to explain many unforeseen incidents, as also some other events of recurring nature. Such views are forcefully transmitted, mostly through their oral traditions from one generation to another. They people know which supernatural force is responsible for what.

During my field work I found that they strongly believe in the evil spirits. The evil spirits or *'Bhut'* today remain an important fact of their life. Also they believe in other aspects of ill fortune as evil eye or *'nazar'*, which they use the same methods to ward off as other evil spirits. These spirits, which live in, the bodies of individual beings and which are controlled by divine hand can be brought under control by '*Ojhas*'. These *Ojhas* are called for expulsion of evil spirits also known as *'jhar-phuk'*.

The religious specialist '*Ojhas*' has a great role to play in guiding the destiny of their community folk. Among various kinds of specialists, at community level, it is the religious ones who import maximum regards. The sacred leaders or specialist continue to have superior position over that secular nature. People's faith for achieving various ends, on the religious persons is superb, and the same is reflected through numerous rituals, ceremonies and practices observed at community level. Many of them, in some other group are explained in a different way which has nothing much to do with this religion.

Economical Status

Their traditional economic activity demonstrates their dependence on the forest. Over time, when this community came in contact with other Hindu societies, they are earth-work, tree cutting dig mud for construction of houses, roads and work in farming fields as laborers, catching rats and other economic activities. In present times they working as landless agricultural labours. They also practice domestication of chickens, Pig, Goat, Cow, Buffalow etc which beside their flesh are also considered useful for their bye products. Along with their traditional works, such as daily wage labour, household worker, working in the brick kiln in the daytime and working to take care of agriculture fields and crops at night.

At present, due to limited employment in the village and daily wages are less, these people has started in search of employment in the outside village or states. At the present time, they seasonally migrated in other state like Punjab, Hariyana and Delhi for agricultural and some other labour work (Singh, 1980; Danda, 1986; Prassad, 1988). Most of the people in the area work in related works related to agricultural works in other states. Some people begin to work there for rickshaw pulling, lifting, Dhabas and hotels. Those who cannot go out for some reason, they do their daily wages in nearby urban areas and raise their families. Due to this reason, some changes come in their life and financially they some improved. Another reason of their economic condition has improved due to the livelihood development programs and schemes being run by government and non-government institutions in the area such as self-help group formation, small cottage industries and employment training programs. Due to the economic condition of Musahar society changes can also be seen in their diet, lifestyle, dress patterns and daily routine etc.

Educational status

They are very less literate. Census, 2011, the total literacy rate of Musahar is 6.88% mark and it is only 3.09% for women. Therefore, they are very backward in every field. During the study researcher show that mostly Musahar children are out of school in the study area. Apparently the educational status of Musahar community is very low (6.8%). Despite international obligations, legal provisions and government initiatives Musahar community has less access to the education. Main cause of less access to the education and low educational status of the Musahar Community is adverse economic condition (poverty) as study a show (Thorat, 2002; Mukhaerjee, 2002; Sharma, 2011, Chauhan, 2013). Due to this reason Musahar parents don't send their children to school. In this study, researcher find out some basic social causes responsible for low education status of Musahar community are lack of awareness on the importance of education, domination upon them, illiteracy among the community, parents early expectation of income from the children, child marriage.

School dropout is very high in Musahar community. The causes of the students drop out is no literate persons at home, due to work other's home, due to take care of siblings at home and graze the cattle and due to involve in labour works then children don't have time do home work and study at home. Apart from this, some other factors also responsible of the students drop out like Teachers behaviors, other caste students behavior, language problem and less interested in study etc.

Government and other non-government agencies takes initiative major steps for uplift their children going to schools likes getting free dress, book, stationary and other goods, opened residential schools, getting scholarship and awareness programs on community level. Due to this initiative effort some Musahar Parents ready to send their children to school.

'Jaati' (Caste) Panchayat of Musahar

Caste Panchayats is very common in traditional Indian Society especially in the village. Most important form of caste Panchayats are known as '*Nyaya*' Panchayats. In the study area, old institutional structure such as Musahar caste Panchayat exist as was the case in the past. Their caste Panchayat play important role in binding the residents in server ways.

According to informant, Panchayat does not have a fixed timeframe to meet. It meets as and when required. As and when problems and issues brought to his notice, and then they swing into action to hold the Panchayat in consultant with other Panchayt members. Generally these caste Panchayats deals with issues, problem and dispute likes quarrels between brothers, family members or neighbour, minor physical fight, disputes arising out of financial transactions within the groups.

In spite of the strong influence of forces of modernization as well as globalization changed his Panchayat institution. Researcher observed during field work that Musahar peoples avail the service of both Catse Panchyat and other government agencies. Major issues such as land disputes and bloody physical fight are taken up by the respective individuals with outside agencies such as police and court of Law.

Change in attitude and Behavioral practices

Various factors involved in the formation of attitude toward changes among the Musahar community. Economic and social mobility are the two main factors influencing their attitudes.

During Field Work I have noted that the many proverb or folk idiom related to Musahar community is popular in the locality. Three of them get the most popular in non- Musahar community. This reflects the character of the Musahar community. First, '*Musahrwa Raja Ja Ta*' (seeing Musahar is walking like a King) the people of other communities say that Musahar people are Capricious. No one can force them to do any work. Second, if someone is fooling anyone, then people say, *'hamra Musahrwa samjhle hai ka?'* (Do you understand me like a Musahar?). Third, if a family member lives in a dirty way rather than being clean, then people say, '*Musaharwa jaisa haal banaile hai*'(Looks like a Musahar). During the field work spending long time with Musahar, observing their daily routine and practices, one I feel that they instantly live in only the present time. Other caste community blamed that Musahar have not time consciousness. It means that they always live in the present. They do not care about future, neither worry about future nor planning for the future.

Suggestion

The government needs to formulate special programs and policies for these people. Income generating and skill generating programs shall be useful for the economic upliftment of this community. Basic health education, adult literacy programs should be introduced to raise their awareness.

If government wants to improve and change their life, the government should take the help of the persons who are having the ethnographical and complete socio-cultural knowledge of the Musahar community. The person should be honest and dedicated towards the real work. This will definitely give positive result.

Establishing a special Gram Sabha for the development of the Musahar community, the participation of the other Scheduled and Backward Castes of the village along with the Musrahar community should be ensured.

Government should Promote the Rat farming: Promotion of rat farming can have great impact on social life of the Musahar Community. Food habits are one of the main factors untouchability. If rat meat is accepted as common food, it would help in bridging the gaps between different communities and would pave way for removal of untouchability. Generally it has been seen that the communities, whose skills have been commercialized have also developed. Musahar community which has the traditional skill of rat hunting has not improved as their skill has not been recognized and commercialized. If we commercialize rat farming, it would definitely have great impact on the poverty alleviation particularly of the communities which are engaged in rat hunting.

The scheduled caste specially Musahar are subject to differential treatment form the government, NGOs and social scientist. The time has come when anthropologist, administrator, politician, and Social worker should come closer and join their hand in the all round development and changes of the these weaker section.

The people of such community for whom welfare scheme will be implemented, should be involvement actively so that they may take special interest. While formulating the scheme by any method the beneficiaries concerned should be allowed to propose their own choice of scheme which will be helpful to them.

Conclusion

Change in the institutional and normative structure of society constitutes social change. It takes place in the field of social relationship (Patnaik, 2008). These include social processes, social pattern and social interactions.

Social Change is the unbreakable rule of creation where all facets of society are transformed. Whether there is any aspect of society, whether it is a social organization or cultural, political or economic aspect, there is interaction in them. And the interconnection remains in them. Therefore, if we also say in the essence, the change in one aspect or part of society means that all other part or aspects change and it can be both positive and negative. Today, where there has been a decrease in interest in their traditional work, social reform among the people of these communities and mass consciousness has been born with many social movements in the nineteenth century. One of the reasons for this would have been that this society was in close contact with local and other external societies due to its inadequacy and engagement in its traditional activities and have continued to live up to its traditional traditions according to its traditional activities. But now, due to the presence of outsiders, local people, in partial change in important societal aspects of various social issues such as caste system, marriage system, family situation, costumes, women's status, relationship, kinship and illiteracy in their society. Together they are also getting loose.

Traditionally, the social, economic, religious and political level of the Scheduled Castes has been extremely low and discriminatory, due to which they have been victims of various religious and social disabilities. The Hindu society has kept them separated from the main social-cultural and religious stream by considering them as intangible and untouchables. The economic condition of these Scheduled Castes has also been extremely low and unsatisfactory due to their traditionally unpopular, disgusting and economically disadvantaged business. Poverty, landlessness, indebtedness, mortgage wages, low wage income, economic exploitation, have been a major reality of social experience of scheduled caste groups.

Researchers have come to the conclusion by research that in the present time where Non-Musahar communities of rural and urban areas are coming in contact with modernity and are progressing on the path of their entire development. In the same place there has been a partial change in the culture and social form of this society, this change is very minor. Modernity has not had much effect on this. Without any hesitation, it can be said that the Musahur community has moved towards some areas in modernity, but in some areas the principles of real society creation are not able to touch them. Due to the development programs and schemes being undertaken by government and non-governmental organizations, these societies should not have been done at that level.

During field work we have found that the developmental efforts of the government and some agencies have contributed positively to uplift the status of the Musahar community. Government effectively implemented of their constitutional safeguards and legal protection of discrimination laws.

The Jaati Panchayat system itself has been found to have brought changes among the Musahar society. Members of the some family therefore migrate to the other places in search of their livelihood. There is no doubt that such migration for their livelihood often leads to mistrust among the family members, kin group, especially, husband and wife, who consequently lead to dispute and divorces too.

The change in family, marriage and kinship are unavoidable aspects in the study of social change, the Musahar strictly practice and follow village exogamy and caste endogamy. However, now changes are occurring in ways of choosing selecting a spouse. Quite often, now spouses are selected keeping in mind their economic stability.

Researchers found that change are taking place in their life, it has increased their social mobility only to some extent, their literacy has increased only to some extent, there is only a slight increased in the coefficient of quality of life and it has slightly improved the inspirational level of Musahar caste peoples.

Poverty among these marginalized castes is not result of a single cause but it is the result of the social, political and economic factors in which marginalized and weak people like Musahars do not have the opportunity to enjoy their basic rights.

Anthropologist's proposal has been proved favourable for implementing any programme for improvement of social economic condition of scheduled caste people including Musahar (Sharma, 2011). Huge amount have been spent over the development of the marginal community the five year plans. They provided better livelihood is one of the main concerns. The land reforms movement and land reclaimed scheme are important but it is in operation in limited area. Due to this land reforms movement some land provided to Musahar people for agriculture purpose in study area. But a very few people get benefitted to this scheme.

References

Aiyappan, A. (1945). 'Iravas and Culture change', Superintendent Government Press, Madras.

Ahuja, Ram (2011). 'Society in India: Concept, Theories and Recent Trends', Rawat Publications, New Delhi.

Arjun Shankar, 2005, *'The Musahars'*, Janki Prakashan, Patna.

Baily, F.G. (1960). 'Political Change in the Kondmals', Rural profile' (ed.) D.N. Majumdar, The ethnography and folk culture Society, Lucknow, U. P.

Beteille, A. (1996) 'Caste, Class and Power: Changing Patterns of Stratification in a Tanjore Village'. University of California Press, Berkeley.

Bhatt, S.C. and Bhargawa, K. (2005). Land and People of Indian State and Union Territories, Vol. Five, Gyan Publishing House, New Delhi.

Blunt, E. A. H. (1969) "The caste system in Northern India", S. Chand & Co., Delhi.

Boskoff, A. (1972). The Mosaic of Sociological Theory. Thomas Y. Crowell Company, New York.

Chauhan, Dinesh 2013, *'Dalit Samaj ki Samashaye'* Rawat Publication, New Delhi (Hindi).

Cohen, Perey S. (1968). 'Modern Social Theory', Heinman Also 1973, edition, London.

Crooke, W. (1896). 'The Tribes and Castes of North-Western Provinces and Oudh' Vol. 3. Office of The supperedented of government Printing, Kolkata.

Danda, A.K. (1986). 'A rural Community in Transition', Intra-India Publications, New Delhi.

Dube , S. C. (1958). 'India's Changing Village', Routledge and Kegan Paul Ltd, London.

Dumont, Lous.1970. Homo Hierarchicus: The Caste System and Its Implications. New Delhi: Oxford University Press.

Goodwin, R. (2009). Changing Relations: Achieving Intimacy in a Time of Social Transition, Cambridge University Press, London.

Ghurye, G.S. 1969. 'Caste and Race in India', Popular Prakashan, Bombay.

Green A. (1952). Sociology: An Analysis of life in Modern Society, McGraw Hill, New York.

Karna, Anamika, 2008, A final report on *"Ethnographic Study of Mushar Community with Emphasis on Female Group: A Case study of Saptary, District, Napal"*, submitted to SIRF Secretariat, SNV Nepal, Bakhundole, Lalitpur, Napal.

Khan, Mumtaz Ali, 1980, *'Scheduled Castes and Their Status in India'*, Uppal Publishing house, New Delhi.

Khare, S. R. 1984. The Untouchable as Himself: Ideology, Identity and Pragmatism among the Lucknow Chamar. Cambridge and New York: Cambridge University Press.

Kuppuswamy, B. (1972). Social Change in India, Vikas Publication, Delhi.

Kumar, Arun, 2006, "Culture, Development and the Cultural Capital of Farce: The Mushar Community in Bihar", Economic and Political Weekly (J), Vol. 41, No. 40 (Oct. 7-13), pp. 4281-4285+4287-4291.

Lockwood, A. (1878). 'Natural History: Sport and Travel', W.H. Allen, London.

Lynch, Owen M. (1969). *The Politics of Untouchability: Social Mobility and Social Change in a City of India,*: Columbia University Press, New York and London.

Maclver, R.M. and Page, C.M. (1953). 'Society', The Macmillan, London.

Malinowski, B. (1958). 'The Dynamic of Culture change', Yale Univeristy press, New York.

Mann, R. S. (1987). 'Social change and Social research', Concept Publishing Company, New Delhi.

Mukul, 1999, "The Untouchable Present: everyday Life of Musahars in North Bihar" Economic and Political Weekly (J), Vol. 34, No.49 (Dec. 4-10), pp. 3465-3470.

Mukhaerjee, Amitav 2002, *'Hunger: Theory Perspective and Reality',* Concept Pub., New Delhi.

Nesufiled, J. C. (1885). Brief view of the system of the north Provinces and Oudh', Allahabad.

Nayak, J. K. (2012). 'Constructive Community Drinking: A Genome Based Socio-cultural Study on Bondo Highlanders' Lambert Academic Publishing, Germany.

O'Malley, L.S.S. (2007) in 'Bihar and Orissa District Gazetteers: Monghyr' (page no -67) Logos Press, New Delhi first published 1926, reprint 2007.

Pandey, K.S. and Sharma, J. (2015). "The Raji Tribe of Uttrakhand in globalized world: In a changing perspective", International Journal of Advanced Research (J), Volume 3, Issue 12, p-84 – 89.

Pokharel, Bhbani. 1997. An Ethnographic Study of the Musahar of Kaji Kovara of Morang district. TU.

Praksah, Nirupma, 1989, "Scheduled Caste: Socio-economic change", Chugh Publication, Allahabad.

Prasad, Anirudh, 1988, "Changing Lifeways and Thoughtway of Musahars in Bodh Gaya", Tradition and Development (Book), Sachichidanada (et.al.), Concept Publication, New Delhi, pp.123-136.

Ranjan, Renu. 1988. 'Tradition and Development Among the Scheduled Caste of Bihar', in ed. book '*Tradition and Development',* by Sachchidananda et. Al., Concept Publishing House, New Delhi, p-107-122.

Risley, H. (1891). 'The Tribe and Caste of Bengal', Bengal Secretariat Press, Culcatta.

Rogers, E. M. (1962). 'Diffusion of Innovations', The free Press of Glenoce, New York.

Rogers, E. M. (1969). 'Modernization among Peasants', Holt, Rinehart and Vinston, New York.

Sachidananda, 1977. *'The Harijan Elite'*, Thomson Press (India) Ltd., Haryana.

Sachichidananda and Lal, A.K., 1979, "Elite and Development", Concept Publication, New Delhi.

Saday, Ram S. (2011). 'Transformation of Identity from Caste Community to Ethnic Group: Agenda of Social Inclusion of Musahar in a Changing Socio-Political Context of Nepal' Report submitted to Matthias Moyersoen Research Apprenticeships, Social Inclusion Research Fund, SIRF Secretariat, SNV Nepal.

Sahu, Chaturbhuj (2009). 'Approaches of Tribal Development' (ed.), Adhyan Publishers and Distribution, New Delhi.

Sen, amartya. 2000. Social Exclusion: Concept, Application and Scrutiny. Social Development Paper No. 1. Manila: ADB.

Sharma J. D. 1998. '*Musahar: Bahu Bhasiya Samaj'* (Hindi), Thakur Prassad Book, Patna.

Sharma, J., Kundu, S. and Mukherjee, A. (2011). "A Caste- Tribe Interaction during a Festival of Sidheswari Puja among Hindu Community in Ballavpur Village (Bolpur) - A Critical Appraisal to Anthropological Perspective" *Vanyajati (J)*, vol. 58, No.04, p. 29-34.

Sharma, J. and Alam, A. (2012). "A Social- Cultural status on Health Development and change among Birhor Tribe of Jharkhand" *Vanyajati (J),* vol.-60, no. 02, p-19-25.

Sharma, J. (2013). "The Socio-economic and Health Status of Rag Picking Children of Small Town (with reference to Hazaribagh Municipal Area)", *The Asian Man (J),* Lucknow, Vol. 07, No. 01 & 02, p- 216-23.

Singh, K.S. (1993). 'The Scheduled Caste; People of India' National Series vol. II, Anthropological Survey of India, Oxford Univeristy Press, Delhi/Kolkata.

Singh, K.S. (1994). 'People of India: Bihar including Jharkhand', Vol. XVI, Part II, Seagull Book, London.

Singh, K.S. 1996. Identity, Ecology, Social Organization, Economy, Linkages and Development Process, a Quantitative Profile, People of India, National Series Vol.VII. Delhi, Oxford University Press.

Singh, Yogendra (1980). 'Social stratification and change in India', Manohar Publishers, Delhi.

Singh, Yogendra (2014). 'Modernization of India Tradition', Rawat Publication, New Delhi.

Sinha, A.N., 2002. The Musahar: A socio-economic Study, Patna. Institute of Social Study, Patna.

Sinha, R., 2005, *Bihar ke Musahara* (B) (Hindi), Janki Prakashan, Patna.

Srinivas, M.N. (1962). 'Caste in Modern India', Asia Publishing House, Bombay.

Srinivas, M.N. (1966). 'Social change in Modern India', Allied publishers, Bombay.

Srinivas, M.N.,Seshiah, S. and Parthasarthy, V.S. (1977). Dimensions of Social change in India. Asia Publishing House, Bombay.

Thorat. S. K. (2002). 'Oppression and Denial: Dalit Discrimination in 1990s', *EPW (J),* New Delhi, *vol.* 37 no. 6, 2002.

Vidyarthi, L.P. and Mishra, N. 1977, "Harijan Today: Sociological, Economic, Political, Religious and cultural analysis, Classical Publication, New Delhi.

Joshua Report (2016). Musahar (Hindu Tradition) in India, Joshua Report (2016). (Web Link:-http://www.joshuaproject.net/people-profile.php).

Census Report, (1981). 'Census of India, Report 1981', New Delhi.

Census Report, (2001). 'Census of India Report 2001', New Delhi.

Census Report, (2011). 'Census of India, Report 2011', New Delhi.

Chapter - 7

An ethnography of food among the Khasis of Wahmaw-Lyngdiar locality of Mawsynram village, East Khasi hills district, Meghalaya

Leena Laskar

Food is our basic need. It is an essential and fundamental part of human society. It is not just a primary factor for survival but food is important for both physical and mental well being. Children and young peoples diet is an important influence on their health now and in the future. It is important that we promote health and demonstrate a positive approach with regard to foods and healthy eating patterns. Food means any substance that people or animals eat or drink or that plants absorb in order to maintain life and growth.

Food is one of the prime necessities of man. All over the world food merely the sources of bio-chemical needs. In every society rice is common food. Food is the carrier of our culture. It represents the identity and cultural richness of a particular society. Food also has a cultural affair, people eat food in a socially organized manner. The staple food of the Khasi people is rice. Apart from rice they take fish and meat. On the ceremonial occasions they love drinking rice-beer. The Khasis are the principal tribal community in the state of Meghalaya.

The Khasis linguistically belong to the Tibeto-Burman groups. The Khasis are the largest tribal community in North East India. The Khasis are inhabited in the East Khasi Hills, West Khasi Hills, Jaintia Hills, and Ri-bhoi districts of Meghalaya. The Khasis who have their habitats in the state of Assam, in Punjab, Uttar Pradesh, Manipur, West Bengal and Jammu and Kashmir have lost many tribe traits. They are called by the different names, such as- Khasi Pahris, Khuchia, Kassi, Khashi and Khasa etc. But a large part of Khasi population is found in the state of Meghalaya.

Objective

The objectives of the research work is to know about the concept of food, food habits, food taboos, food restrictions, food preservation, rules of eating food, food preparation methods and also the food restrictions during pregnancy and sickness period among the Khasis of Wahmaw-Lyngdiar locality.

Methodology

Methodology refers to the methods, techniques or tools which are employed for the collection and processing of data. But in a broader sense methods or techniques are one of the key components of methodology.

The study is an attempt to present such an interesting aspect to the readers especially through a succinct account of the study area. The study was conducted in the Wahmaw-Lyngdiar locality of Mawsynram village, East Khasi Hills District Meghalaya in the month of February, 2017. The data was collected through primary data collection among the people of Wahmaw-Lyngdiar locality. Another methods used during data collection were Interview method, Observation method, Schedule method, Photographic method method.

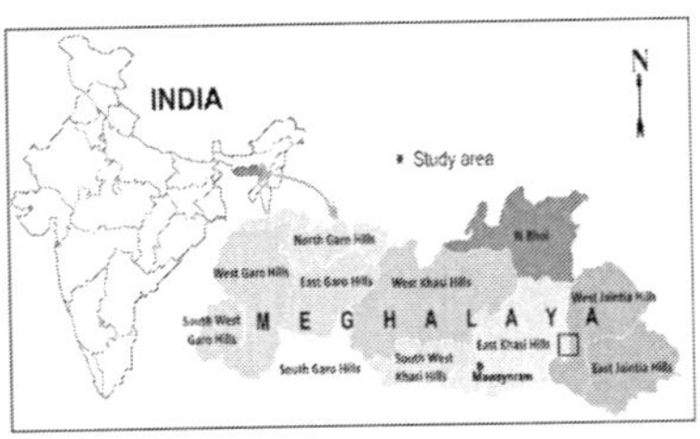

Fig. 1: Map of Meghalaya

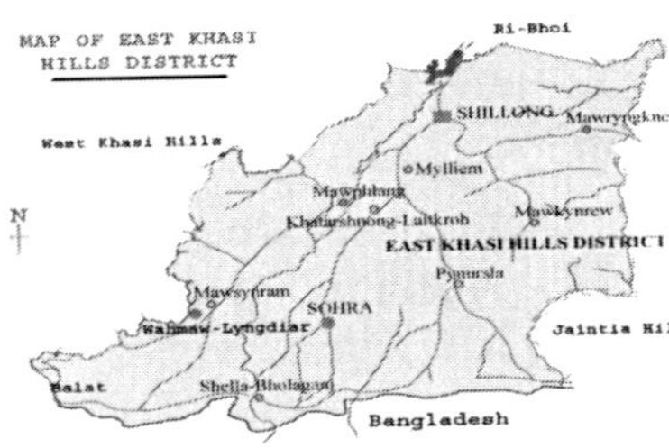

Fig. 2: Map of East Khasi Hills District

Study Area

The area where study was conducted is Wahmaw-Lyngdiar locality of Mawsynram village in East Khasi Hills District, Meghalaya. Wahmaw-Lyngdiar is a small locality, which is consisted of 24 Households of indigenous Khasi people. It is about 2 kilometers away from Mawsynram village and 67 kilometers far from state capital Shillong. In the east of this locality Lawbah and Ryngku are situated. In west Balat is located. Laitsohum and Phudphandlei are situated in the south, and in the north Mawsynram village is situated.

The name *Wahmaw-Lyngdiar* was given by the people of this locality. The term *'Wahmaw-Lyngdiar'* is a Khasi root word, which is formed by two words *'Mawbah'* and *'Lyngdiar'*. *'Mawbah'* means '*huge rock*' and 'Lyngdiar' means *'habitation'*. Therefore the term *Wahmaw-Lyngdiar* means- *a habitation near or below a huge rock.* In this locality, people have been living since 1975

The village Mawsynram receives 467 inches of rain per year. Mawsynram is situated in a subtropical highland with an extraordinarily showery and long monsoon season and a short dry season.The village Mawsynram receives 11,872 milimeters of rain per year. The area is quite cold and breezy. There are different kinds of vegetations around the village area.

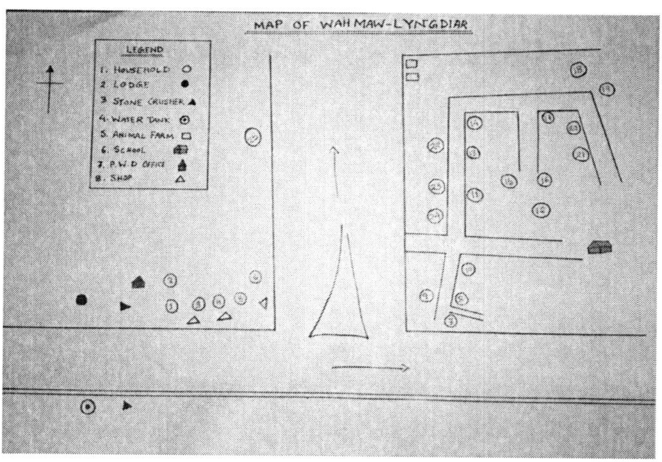

Fig. 3: Map of Study Area

Table No. 1: Family type of the Locality

Type	*Number*	*%*
Nuclear	8	33.33
Extended	1	4.17
Joint	5	20.83
Incomplete	10	41.67
Total	24	100.00

Source: Fieldwork, 2017

Plate 1: Entrance of the Locality

Plate 2: Key Informent and reseracher wearing Khasi Traditional Attire

Plate 3: Intrepreter

Plate 4: Natural Environment of the Study Area

Results and Discussion

The Khasis ordinarily take two meals a day, one in the early morning and the other in the evening, but labourers and others who have to work hard in the open, they take a midday meal as well, consisting of cold boiled rice wrapped in a leaf, known as *Ka-já-song,* cakes- *ki kpu* and a tuberous root, called *u-sohphlang*, which is eaten raw. Khasis are fond of all kinds of meat, especially pork and beef, although some of the Seng Khasis, owing to Hindu influence, abstain from eating the latter. The Khasis do not eat the flesh of dog. Because there is a Khasi folk-tale relating how the dog came to be regarded as the friend of man. It is, however, quite possible that the Khasi people may never have eaten the flesh of the dog from remote times. The staple food of the Khasis is rice and dried fish.When rice cannot be obtained or is scarce, millet or Job's tears are used instead of rice. Khasis eat the flesh of nearly all wild animales; they also eat field rats and one kind of monkey, known as*u-shrih.* The Khasis consider a curry made from a kind of green frog, called *ka-japieh*, a bonne bouche. They however do not eat ordinary frogs, called as *jakoid* (Gurdan, T.R.P. Reprint 2012, pp. 51-52).

A staple food which must not be forgotten is the inner portion of the bark of the sago plam tree, known as *ka-tlái,* which grows wild in the forest and attains a large size. The tree is felled and the outer bark removed, the soft inner part is cut into slices, dried in the sun, pounded in a mortar and then passed through a fine bamboo sieve. Reddish flour is obtained, of sweet taste, which is boiled with rice. This flour is good for making cakes and puddings.

The Khasis are in the habit of regularly drinking considerable quantities of rice-beer. Among the Khasis there are two kinds of rice-beer, namely- *ka'iad hiar* and *ka'iad um.* Both of these are made from rice and in some places these are made from millet and the root of a plant called *u-khawiang.* *Ka'iad hiar* is made by boiling the rice or millet. *Ka'iad hiar* is said to be stronger than *ka'iad um.*

Rules of Eating Food among the Khasis

Khasi people follow some rules, when they are eating food. They take their food with right hand only. The Khasi children are not permitted to talk when they take their meal but they can talk with elder one when they wantextra food. After finishing their meal they have to wash their hands and then they can drink the water. They eat betel nut with betel leaf or *kwai-tympew* after their meal.

Five Special Foods among the Khasis

The Khasis have five special foods. Such as:-*Jadoh, Ja Stem, Tungrymbai, Dohneiiong* and *Dohkhlieh.*

Jadoh: This is a typical food among the Khasis. It is a mixture of rice with pork or sometimes cooked with chicken and fish. It includes spices like onion, garlic, turmeric and ginger. It gives a slight taste of Biryani but less spicy.

Plate 5: Jadoh

Ja Stem: Ja Stem is another favorite food of Khasis. It is cooked from rice and turmeric powder which makes it yellow in colour. It is also cooked with black sesame seed to further enhance the flavor.

Plate 6: Ja Stem

Tungrymbai: Tungrymbai is prepared from fermented soya beans and a mixture of other spices. It is one kind of chatni which is highly delicious and found almost in every Khasi food stall.

Plate 7: Tungrymbai

Dohneiiong: This dish is a mixture of pork and black sesame seeds. Although, it is simple in cooking but theflavor of the sesame seeds adds another taste to the dish that makes it mouth-watering.

Plate 8: Dohneiiong

Dohkhlieh: Dohkhlieh, which is another popular cuisine among the Khasis, includes boiled pork, onions and chilies.

Plate 9: Dohkhlieh

Food Restrictions among the Khasis

The Khasis have some food restrictions during pregnancy and illness period. For example:

- The pregnant women are not permited to take alcohal, sour and bitter food items.
- When Khasi people suffer from illness like diarrhea and dysentery, they avoid some food items such as- Pork, Oily food, Spicy food and Tungrymbai etc.
- Khasi people do not eat egg when they are suffering from fever.

Food Taboos among the Khasis

The Khasi people love to eat various types of food. In generally, Khasi people do not have any food taboos. But among the some clans they have food taboo or *sang*. They are as follows-

- The Cherra Siem family cannot eat dried fishor khá-piah.
- The Siemof Mylliem must not eat the gourd or u-patháw.
- Some of the Siemlieh class does not eat a fish, calledka'khá-lani.
- The Wár people must not eat preserved fish or ka-ktung.
- The'khar-um-núid clan of Khyrimis prohibited from eating pork.
- The 'dkhar clan cannot eat the meat of the sow but they can eat the meat of male pig.

Areca nut performs one special rule in their day-to-day life. The Khasis are warm hearted people. Their gesture of friendship is offering Betel nut or *Kwai* to their friends for every visit.

Plate 10: How Khasis stored Betel Leaves and Areca Nuts

Plate 11: How offering Areca nuts as a symbol of gesture.

Plate 12: Betel Leaves and Areca Nuts wrapped in Turmeric Leaf for selling purpose

Foods Having during Breakfast

Khasi breakfast is mainly prepared from rice. They love to eat rice based foods. Some propular breakfast among the Khasis are Putharo, Pukhlein, Pusongsla, Pusyep, Pu-maloi, Pudoh, Punei, Pujer, Pusaw, Pukhadu, Pusyrtap, Jingbam Khaw, Red Potato, Tapioca etc.

Plate 13: Putharo, Pukhlein, Pusongsla

Plate 14: Jingbam Khaw or Rice Cake

Plate 15: A Khasi woman preparing Pu-maloi

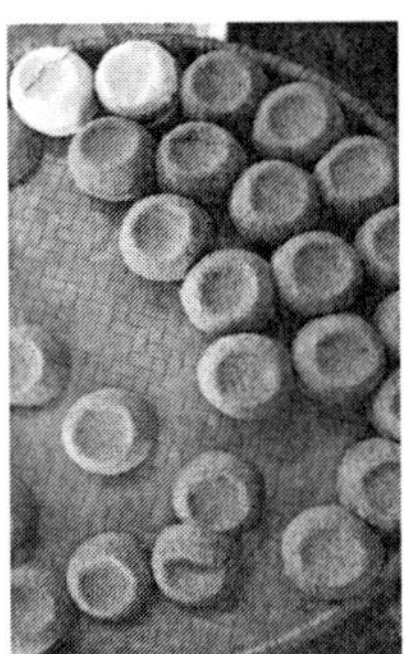

Plate 16: Pu-maloi

Plate 17: Pu-maloi preparing process

Plate 18: Boiled Tapioca or Phandi

Plate 19: Red Potato or Phan-saw

Foods Having during Leisure

Khasi peoples are always busy in different agricuitural activities. During leisure period they having different types of local foods like Sohling (it looks like Jackfruit Seeds, which is found only in Meghalaya), U-Sohphlang (A tuberous root, which is eaten raw. Teaste is slight sour) etc.

Plate 20: Sohling (It looks like Jackfruit Seeds, which is found only in Meghalaya)

Plate 21: U-Sohphlang (A tuberous root, which is eaten raw. Teaste is slight sour)

Table 2: Khasi terminology of popular food

Local Name	*English Name*
Khaw	Rice
Jingbam Khaw	Rice Cake
Mlush	Salt
Umphniang	Mustard Oil

(Contd...)

Piat	Onion
Sohmarit	Black Pepper
Shayrmit	Turmeric
Sohsaw	Tomato
Doh	Meat
Doh Khosdieh	Dry Fish
Rynsun	Garlic
Sying	Ginger
Sohkhia	Cucumber
Phan	Potato
Neiiong	Sesame
Kyied Ym	Rice Wine
Shriew	Yam
Kwai	Betel Nut
Tympew	Betel Leaf
Siej	Bamboo

Conclusion

From the study it has been found that the staple food of the Khasis is rice. Apart from rice they love to eat fish and meat. On the ceremonial occasions they love drinking rice-beer. Among the Khasis there are two kinds of rice-beer, namely- ka'iad-um and ka'iad hiar.The Khasis have five special foods namely- Jadoh, Ja-Stem, Tungrymbai, Dohneiiong, and Dohkhleih. Khasi society has some rules of eating. In generally, Khasi people do not have any food restriction and food taboos. But during illness and pregnancyperiod they obey some food restrictions. Among the Khasis food taboos are not found as a whole, it founds only in some particular clans. Such as- The Cherra Siem family, Siem of Mylliem, Siemlieh class, Wár people, 'Khar-um-núid clan of Khyrim and 'Dkhar clan.

Acknowledgement

It is an immene privilege for me to convey my thanks to those who helped me during the course of research work. My special thanks goes to the people of *Wahmaw-Lyngdiar* locality for their endless help, co-operation and warm hospitality, without which my mission would not have been possible. I am grateful particularly to Mr. Moonstar Marbaniang, Head-man or *Rongbah-Shong* of Mawsynram village for his co-operation and permission to carry out the research work. I also thank Mr. Naros Marbaniang, the *Rongbah-Dong* of *Wahmaw-Lyngdiar* Locality. I would like to convey my heartfelt thanks to Mr. Kit Bok Lang Lyngdoh, the owner of the Rit-Mawksyr Lodge for his warm hospitality, where I stayed during study period. Last but not the least I take this opportunity to thank my parents for their financial help and co-operation.

References

Bose, J. K.1980. *Glimpses of Tribal Life in North-East India*. Calcutta: Institute of Social Research and Applied Anthropology.

Das, J. N. 1990. *A Study of Land System of Meghalaya*. Guwahati: Law Research Institute, Eastern Region.

Gurdon, P. R. T. 2012 (Reprint). *The Khasis*. New Delhi: Akansha Publishing House.

Hans, Raj. 2013 (reprint). *Theory and Practice in Social Research*. New Delhi: Surjeet Publications.

Kothari, C. R. 2017 (Reprint). *Research Methodology Methods and Techniques*. New Delhi: New age International publishers Pvt. Ltd.

Murcott, A. 1982. *The Cultural Significance of Food and Eating*. Cambridge University Press.

Nongrum, Melari Shisha. And Dohtdong, Laribha. July 2018. Changes in the Consumption of Traditional Food among the Khasi and Jaintia People in Rural Meghalaya, India.

International Journal of Food and Nutritional Science (IJFANS): Vol. 7, No. 3.

Umdor, Magdaline. Kyndiah, Eugenia. and Mawlong, Hilda Mary Lyngdoh. June 2016.

Indigenous Knowledge In Preparing Rice Based Foods By The Tribes Of Meghalaya.

International Journal of Innovative Research and Advanced Studies (IJIRAS): Volume 3, Issue 7.

Upadhyay, V. S. 1997, 2016 (reprint). *History of Anthropological Thought*. New Delhi: Concept Publishing Company.

Chapter - 8

Socio-demographic determinants and their effects on Infant mortality among two tribal population groups of Dhemaji districts, Assam, Northeast India

Milonjyoti Borgohain

Infant death is strongly associated with national socio-economic development and it is considered to be a sensitive indicator of socio-economic and health situations prevailing in a community (Antonovsky and Bernestein 1977). Socio-economic development of a state is often reflected by the existing infant mortality rates. The study of infant mortality gets importance, especially because mortality during the first year of life is invariably high for all countries. In India, more or less 1.72 million children die every year prior to reaching their first birthday. It is not only a foremost target but also an important strategy to realize health for everyone. It is worth mentioning that, India has experienced a remarkable decline in infant deaths since the 1970s. India has made vital actions in reducing in infant and under-five mortality i.e., 40/1000 and 52/1000 live births respectively, but it has been unable to achieve the Millennium Development Goal (MDG) by 2015 (Bhaumik S. 2013).

A good number of studies have scrutinized concerning the influence of socio-economic and demographic variables on child endurance (Das Gupta, 1990).It was found that where female literacy is low, infant death rates tend to be very high. Several studies showed that mother's education, birth order, age of the mother, place of delivery, sex of the child, place of residence, religion, income, standard of living etc. are the core determinants of infant death.

Materials and Methods

Location of the area of study and sample population

The materials for the present study was collected in the homogenous Mising and Deori villages namely Lakhipather *Mising* Gaon and Kapahtali Deori Gaon located at Dhemaji District, Assam, India. It falls under Sissiborgaon Development Block, Dhemaji District, Assam.*

Sample size

A total of 200 subjects of which 100 ever married Mising mothers (15-49 years) from Lakhipather *Mising* Gaon and 100 ever married Deori mothers (15-49 years) from Kapahtali Deori Gaon with at least one living child are interviewed for the purpose of the infant mortality.

The data were collected primarily through personal interviews by using structured schedules. The data in the present study was analyzed by using standard statistical techniques and different statistical measures.

Objectives

The specific objectives of the study are as follows:

To examine the level of infant mortality and identify the socio-demographic determinants of infant mortality among the Misings and Deoris of Dhemaji district, Assam, Northeast India.

Results and Discussion

Studies of infant mortality reveal that a few socio- demographic variables have certain impact on infant death. The distributions of infant mortality by demographic and socio-economic variables are discussed as follows:

Tables 1A and 2A shows the sex-wise distribution of infant mortality in various age groups of women. The result showed that the overall

Table 1 A: Sex-wise distribution of infant mortality in various age groups of Mising women

Present age group of women (years)	*No. of women*	*No. of live births*	*Infant deaths*					
			Male		*Female*		*Total*	
			No.	*%*	*No.*	*%*	*No.*	*%*
15-19	28	72	5	6.94	4	5.56	9	12.5
20-24	35	110	7	6.36	3	2.73	10	9.09
25-29	32	92	7	7.61	5	5.43	12	13.04

* Please see map of Assam & map of Dhemaji District at page 107

(Contd...)

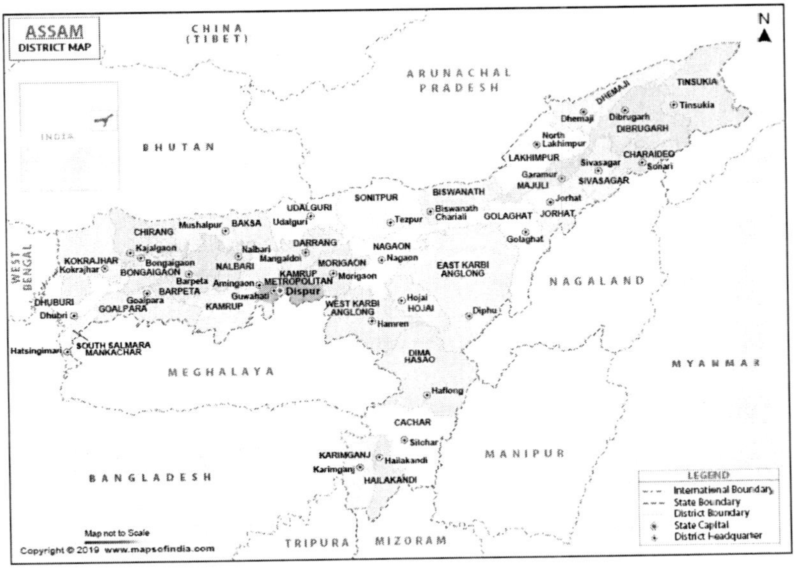

Fig 1: Map of Assam

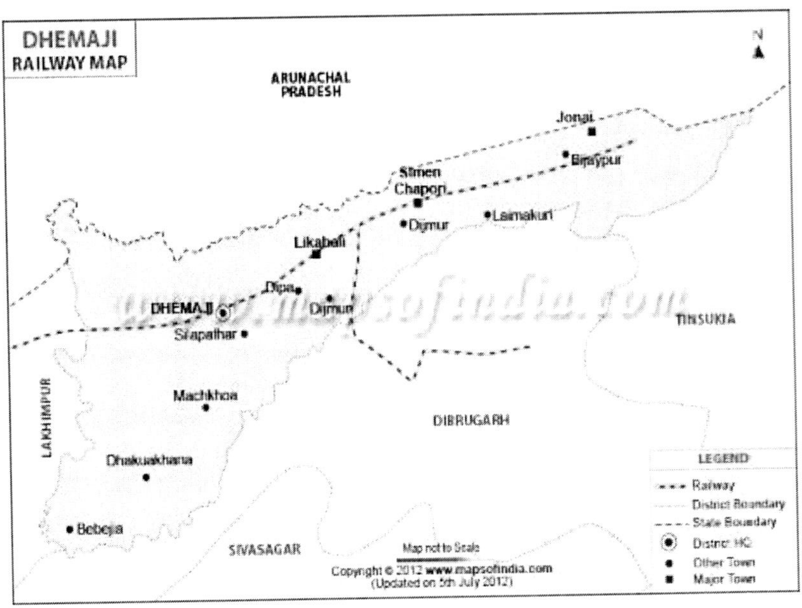

Fig 2: Map o f Dhemaji District

30-34	24	80	9	11.25	4	5.00	13	16.25
35-39	28	88	11	12.5	7	7.95	18	20.45
40-44	29	128	14	10.94	13	10.16	27	21.09
45-49	26	122	16	13.11	14	11.48	30	24.59
Total	200	692	69	9.97	50	7.23	119	17.19

Table 2A: Sex-wise distribution of infant mortality in various age groups of Deori women

Present age group of women (years)	*No. of women*	*No. of live births*	*Infant deaths*					
			Male		*Female*		*Total*	
			No.	*%*	*No.*	*%*	*No.*	*%*
15-19	32	110	11	10.00	4	3.63	15	13.63
20-24	30	96	6	6.25	6	6.25	12	12.5
25-29	33	112	8	7.14	9	8.03	17	15.18
30-34	23	65	7	10.77	7	10.77	14	21.54
35-39	30	111	10	9.00	11	9.90	21	18.92
40-44	24	81	7	8.64	7	8.64	14	17.28
45-49	28	107	11	10.28	5	4.67	16	14.95
Total	200	682	60	8.79	49	7.18	109	15.98

percentage of infant death is relatively higher among the Misings (16.33%) then that of the Deoris (15.98%). The table also shows that the male infant mortality is higher than that of the female infant mortality in both of the populations. The percentages of infant mortality tend to increase with the increasing age groups of the mothers in both the populations. Moreover, it is observed that the incidence of male infant mortality (13.11%) was higher among the Mising women of aged (45-49) years whereas in Deoris, it was 10.28% at the same age group.

Distribution of infant mortality rate is presented in the table 3A. The table shows that the infant mortality rates are quite higher among the Misings (17.19%) than that of the Deoris (15.98%). It is also evident that the neo-natal and post neonatal mortality rates are higher among the Misings as well as among the Deoris.

Infant mortality according to birth order is presented in the table 3B. It is evident from the table that the highest birth order among the Misings and Deoris are found to be six (06). It is important that the percentages of infant mortality are found to increase particularly from the 2nd birth order to higher birth order in both the populations. The highest percentage of infant death is found in the 6th birth order in both the populations, and the percentages are 32.76 and 23.21 respectively. The lowest percentage of infant death is observed in the 2nd birth order (9.09%) followed by 3rd birth order (13.07%) among the Misings, whereas, the lowest percentage of infant death is observed in the 1st birth order (12.00%) followed by 2nd birth order (12.06%).

Tables 1B and 2B shows the infant death according to the educational status among the Mising and Deori couples. From the tables, it is observed

Table IB Infant mortality according to educational status of Mising couples

Wives' educational status	*Husbands' educational status*														
	Illiterate			*Primary up to class viii*			*Class ix to class xii*			*Graduate and above*			*Total*		
	No of couples	*No of live birth*	*No of infant death*	*No of couples*	*No of live birth*	*No of infant death*	*No of couples*	*No of live birth*	*No of infant death*	*No of couples*	*No of live birth*	*No of infant death*	*No of couples*	*No of live birth*	*No of infant death*
Illiterate	20	112	19 (16.96)	21	98	23 (23.46)	13	68	9 (13.24)	-	-	-	54	278	51 (18.35)
Primary up to class viii	22	68	11 (16.17)	28	101	13 (12.87)	19	72	9 (12.5)	3	12	4 (33.33)	72	253	37 (51.39)
Class ix to class xii	18	42	8 (19.05)	20	33	9 (27.27)	16	42	5 (11.90)	9	21	5 (23.80)	65	138	27 (19.57)
Graduate and above	-	-	-	7	18	4 (22.22)	-	-	-	4	5	-	9	15	4 (26.67)
Total	60	222	38	76	250	49 (19.6)	48	182	23 (12.64)	16	38	9 (23.68)	200	692	119 (17.19)

Table 2B Infant mortality according to educational status of Deori couples

Wives' educational status	*Husbands' educational status*														
	Illiterate			*Primary up to class viii*			*Class ix to class xii*			*Graduate and above*			*Total*		
	No of couples	*No of live birth*	*No of infant death*	*No of couples*	*No of live birth*	*No of infant death*	*No of couples*	*No of live birth*	*No of infant death*	*No of couples*	*No of live birth*	*No of infant death*	*No of couples*	*No of live birth*	*No of infant death*
Illiterate	23	108	12 (11.11)	20	80	13 (16.25)	18	62	11 (11.74)	8	23	5 (21.74)	69	273	41 (15.01)
Primary up to class viii	18	42	6 (14.28)	27	110	19 (17.27)	17	56	9 (16.07)	6	11	3 (27.27)	68	219	37 (16.89)
Class ix to class xii	17	68	9 (13.24)	23	62	11 (17.74)	13	32	6 (18.75)	4	7	-	57	169	26 (15.38)
Graduate and above	-	-	-	4	16	5 (31.25)	2	5	-	-	-	-	6	21	5 (23.80)
Total	58	218	27 (12.38)	74	268	48 (17.91)	50	155	26 (16.77)	18	41	8 (19.51)	200	682	109 (15.98)

that the number of infant mortality reduces with the rising educational status of both Mising and Deori couples. The highest percentage of infant mortality among the Misings is revealed by the pairs where they are illiterate (16.96%), followed by the pairs where the husbands and wives are studied primary to class 8th standard and the percentage is 16.17. It is worth mentioning that the couples studied up to class 9th standard to class 12th standard and graduate couples shows the lowest percentage of infant mortality among the Misings. The same scenario is observed among the Deori couples.

Table 1C and 2C shows the infant death according to occupational status of Mising and Deori coupes. It is clear from the table that among the Mising couples with cultivators show the highest percentage of infant mortality (20.69%) followed by the couples engaged with skilled worker husbands and petty business wives (19.04%). On the other hand, the lowest percentage of infant death is found among the couples with petty business (5.56%).

On the other hand, among the Deoris, the couples with cultivator husbands and petty business wives show the highest percentage of infant death (44.83%) followed by the couples with cultivator husbands and wives are engaged in skilled worker (38.89%). Whereas, the lowest percentage of infant death is found among the pairs in which both the husbands and wives are petty businessman (7.14%) followed by the pairs in which husbands are petty businessman and wives are engaged in cultivation (11.32%). It is obvious that the pairs in which both the husbands and wives are engaged in petty businessman show comparatively lower percentage of infant death in both the population groups.

Attendant at the time of delivery is also an important determinant of child survival. It is important to note that, infant mortality is found to be higher among the Misings when deliveries are performed by the untrained persons (57.98%). It is evident that 42.02 percent when deliveries are conducted by doctors and well trained nurses. Whereas, among the Deoris, 49.54 percent infant deaths when deliveries are performed by untrained persons. And 50.46 percent when deliveries are conducted by trained doctors and nurses. Thus, it is clear that doctors and well trained nurses are required for harmless child birth as well as mothers.

Various symptoms and causes of infant mortality among the Misings and Deoris are shown in the table 5. From the table it is clear that the foremost cause of infant death is stomach problems (33.61%) followed by other infections (19.33%) among the Misings. Whereas, it is observed that stomach problems (29.36%), mainly diarrhoea is the prime cause of infant

Table 1C Infant mortality according to occupational status of Mising couples

Wives' occupational status	*Husbands' occupational status*														
	Cultivator			*Skilled worked*			*Petty business*			*Government service*			*Total*		
	No of couples	*No of live birth*	*No of infant death*	*No of couples*	*No of live birth*	*No of infant death*	*No of couples*	*No of live birth*	*No of infant death*	*No of couples*	*No of live birth*	*No of infant death*	*No of couples*	*No of live birth*	*No of infant death*
Cultivator	114	374	78 (20.69)	10	42	6 (14.28)	7	34	5 (14.70)	-	-	-	131	454	89 (19.60)
Skilled worked	9	40	5 (12.5)	6	18	2 (11.11)	4	20	3 (15.00)	12	40	5 (12.5)	31	118	15 (12.71)
Petty business	11	26	4 (15.38)	9	21	4 (19.04)	4	18	1 (5.56)	6	29	2 (6.89)	30	94	11 (11.70)
Government service	6	20	3 (15.00)	2	6	1 (16.67)	-	-	-	-	-	-	8	26	4 (15.38)
Total	140	464	90 (19.39)	27	87	13 (14.94)	15	72	9 (12.5)	18	69	7 (10.14)	200	692	119 (17.19)

Table 2c Infant mortality according to occupational status of Deori couples

Wives' occupational status	*Husbands' occupational status*														
	Cultivator			*Skilled worked*			*Petty business*			*Government service*			*Total*		
	No of couples	*No of live birth*	*No of infant death*	*No of couples*	*No of live birth*	*No of infant death*	*No of couples*	*No of live birth*	*No of infant death*	*No of couples*	*No of live birth*	*No of infant death*	*No of couples*	*No of live birth*	*No of infant death*
Cultivator	98	356	42 (11.79)	17	57	13 (22.80)	15	53	6 (11.32)	3	12	2 (16.67)	133	478	63 (13.18)
Skilled worked	11	36	14 (38.89)	9	28	10 (35.71)	10	35	5 (14.28)	-	-	-	30	99	29 (29.29)
Petty business	9	29	13 (44.83)	6	13	-	12	42	3 (7.14)	2	5	-	29	89	16 (17.98)
Government service	2	7	1 (14.28)	-	-	-	-	-	-	6	9	-	8	16	1 (6.25)
Total	120	428	70 (16.35)	32	98	23 (23.47)	37	130	14 (10.77)	11	26	2 (7.69)	200	682	109 (15.98)

Table 3A: Distribution of infant mortality rate of the Misings and Deoris

Populations	*No. of live births*	*Infant mortality rates*		
		Neo-natal	*Post neo-natal*	*Total*
Misings	692	53 (7.65%)	66 (9.54%)	119 (17.19%)
Deoris	682	46(6.74%)	63 (9.24%)	109 (15.98%)

Table 3B: Infant mortality according to birth order of Misings and Deoris

Birth order	*Misings*			*Deoris*		
	No. of live birth	*Infant death*		*No. of live birth*	*Infant death*	
		No.	*%*	*No.*	*No.*	*%*
1	152	21	13.82	150	18	12.00
2	143	13	9.09	141	17	12.06
3	130	17	13.07	128	19	14.84
4	118	24	20.34	116	22	18.96
5	91	25	27.47	91	20	21.98
6	58	19	32.76	56	13	23.21
7	-	-	-	-	-	-
Total	692	119	17.19	682	109	15.98

Table 3C: Infant mortality according to educational status of Misings and Deori women

Wives' educational status	*Misings*			*Deoris*		
	No of women	*No of live birth*	*No of infant death*	*No of women*	*No of live birth*	*No of infant death*
Illiterate	54	278	51 (18.35)	69	273	41 (15.01)
Primary up to class viii	72	253	37 (51.39)	68	219	37 (16.89)
Class ix to class xii	65	138	27 (19.57)	57	169	26 (15.38)
Graduate and above	9	15	4 (26.67)	6	21	5 (23.80)
Total	200	692	119 (17.19)	200	682	109 (15.98)

Table 4: Distribution of infant mortality attendant at the time of delivery

Attendant at the time of delivery	*Misings*		*Deoris*	
	No.	*%*	*No.*	*%*
Trained doctors and nurses	50	42.02	55	50.46
Untrained persons	69	57.98	54	49.54
Total	119	100	109	100

Table 5: causes and symptoms of infant death

Causes and symptoms	*Misings*		*Deoris*	
	No.	*%*	*No.*	*%*
Stomach problems	40	33.61	32	29.36
Accurate Respiratory Infection (ARI)	21	17.65	21	19.27
Cough and fever	15	12.60	17	15.59
Jaundice	13	10.92	15	13.76
Other infections	23	19.33	19	17.43
Caused not identified	07	5.88	05	4.59
Total	119	100	109	100

death among the Deoris. However, it is also mentioned that Accurate Respiratory Infection (ARI) is an important cause of infant death among both the populations and the percentages are 17.65 and 19.27 respectively. The main causes and symptoms described by the couples are as mentioned-

Causes	*Symptoms*
Stomach problem	Diarrhoea, pain, loose motion, food poisoning.
Jaundice	Yellow colour of skin and red of the eyes.
Cough and fever	Cough, fever, cold, vomiting
Accurate Respiratory Infections (ARI)	Unable to breadth after birth, unable to cry after birth.
Other infections	Infections due to unhygienic removal of the umbilical cord by using old blades, knife, and bamboo splinter.

Table 6 shows the distribution of infant mortality by place of delivery. This table reveals that most of the deliveries of both the population groups take place at home with the help of untrained persons who used to cut the umbilical cord with help of knife or blade.

Table 6: Distribution of infant death by place of delivery

Place of delivery	Misings		Deoris		Total	
	No.	%	No.	%	No.	%
Government hospitals	32	26.89	37	33.94	69	30.26
Private nursing home	11	9.24	13	11.93	24	10.53
Home	76	63.87	59	54.13	135	59.21
Total	119	100	109	100	228	100

Conclusion

This study is based on the data collected from Mising and Deoris inhabited from the Dhemaji district of Assam, Northeast India.

The overall percentage of infant mortality is quite higher among the Mising women (17.19%). Moreover, the incidence of male infant death is higher than that of the female infant death among both the populations.

The major cause of infant death is found to be stomach problems, mainly diarrhoea both among the Misings and Deoris.

The present study exposes that, most of the deliveries of the Misings and Deoris take place at home with the help of untrained persons who used to cut the umbilical cord with the help of knife or blade. Therefore, absence of doctor and trained nurse is also an important factor of infant death. It is worth mentioning that the gap between the two births is one of the prime factors of infant death. Maternal education is another important finding where infant mortality is found to higher in comparison to that of the educated mother. Early and late marriage of women is another prime cause of high infant death; however, we can't expect a healthy baby which has experimentally been proved by the field survey.

References

Antonovsky A. And Bernstein J., 1977, "Social Class and Infant Mortality", *Social Science and Medicine*, Volume-11, Issues 8-9, Pages 453-470.

Bhaumk S. 2013, "Child mortality: will India achieve the 2015 target?", *BMJ*; 346: f1502.

Das Gupta, 1990, "Death Clustering, Nother's Education and Determinants of child Mortality in Rural Punjab, India", *Population Studies,* 44, 489-505.

Chapter - 9

A study on unpropitious women entrepreneurship in *japi* making activity: a case study of Nalbari district, Assam

Nibedita Choudhury

Entrepreneurship plays a crucial role in the economic growth of a country. A. Schumpeter first described the process of entrepreneurship by putting human agents at the core of economic development and also defines as the use of a novel combination of the available means of production. According to him, "Entrepreneurship" refers to a process ad "Entrepreneurs" are the innovators who use the process for innovating new business (Desai:7). The term "Entrepreneur" is not gender-specific. Thus, it also embraces both men and women. The government of India defines "Women Entrepreneurship" as an enterprise having a maximum of 51% financial capital and generating a minimum of 51% employment for women. In the current scenario, in India, more and more women have started engaging in various enterprises and hence, it can be said that women entrepreneurship now on the verge of transformation (Baporikar:75). However, in spite of having huge potentialities, women entrepreneurship is still underdeveloped in many parts of India particularly among *Japi* manufacturing cluster of Assam.

Japi making activity is a traditional activity which is taken by some section of Assamese society as their profession. *Japi* is the traditional headgear used by the people of Assam. Assamese society is traditionally an agriculture-based society and its economy run by agriculture. In this case, *Japi* as a material is used as headgear in the agricultural fields in order to protect from rain and strong sun rays. Being used as a headgear without any supporting hands to it, it is quite comfortable to use while working in the agricultural fields. It is also used as an honoring item in order to pay tribute to the receiver. Further, *Japi* is used for decorative purposes as well as in Bihu dances. Therefore, *Japi* has also gained recognition as a great symbol of Assamese culture and society. Nalbari, Kamrup, Nagaon, Darrang, Sivsagar, and Lakhimpur are some of the prominent centers known for their *Japi* making industry. According to the report of Commissionerate of Industries and Commerce, Government of Assam 2018, among these centers some of the villages of Nalbari district are known as the center of excellence. In this regard, Tilana village of Nalbari district is worth mentioning. For a long time, the people of this village have been engaged with this tradition. They export their products to different places of Assam. This has been the primary occupation of most of the people of these villages. In the village Tilana, there are a few local entrepreneurs who conduct *Japi* making activity. However, the status of entrepreneurship is not satisfactory and mostly dominated by males. Women help in various stages of *Japi* manufacturing activity. But, they are hardly encouraged to get themselves involved in the entrepreneurial activities in *Japi* making.

Literature Review

Several studies on women entrepreneurship have been done so far. Various scholars have studied women entrepreneurial activities from various perspectives. Moore and Buttner (1997) have talked about female entrepreneurship, the relationship between women and organizational life, etc. Hence, the study further states the difficulties faced by the women entrepreneurs and also made some suggestions for the betterment of future entrepreneurs.

Rao (2011) highlights the problems of women entrepreneurship in India. He explained women entrepreneurial activities in the Indian context and explained well various challenges lingering in women entrepreneurship. Kumar (2017) also talks about the problems of women entrepreneurship in micro, small and medium enterprises and also mentions various government schemes associated with women empowerment. Goyal and Prakash (2011) have beautifully described the process of women entrepreneurship, various reasons for the slow pace of women entrepreneurs in India with special reference to the women entrepreneurs of Ludhiana and made suggestions for the betterment of the same. Sugaraj and Salve P.S (2014) explains the problems associated with women entrepreneurship in Western Maharastra such as poor self-images, lack of finance, lack of motivation, role conflicts and so on.

However, the above studies have lacked in the explanation of the importance of the women entrepreneurial activities in *Japi* making tradition.

Hence, the present study will try to cover women entrepreneurship in *Japi* making activity.

Statement of the Problem

Although, studies on women entrepreneurship in micro, small scale, and medium scale industries have been done in a significant number, yet there has been a paucity of studies on women's entrepreneurial development in *Japi* making tradition specifically. Due to the negligence of women entrepreneurship in *Japi* making tradition, despite having huge potentialities most of the women of the study village are still not independent. The present study will attempt to investigate various problems that have been creating obstacles in entrepreneurship development among women. In this regard, people's perspective will be helpful to understand the present condition of the women entrepreneurship in *Japi* making tradition and the reasons that have forced these entrepreneurial opportunities to show a decline in its growth.

Objective of the Study

(1) To examine the women entrepreneurship in Japi making activity and the socio-economic condition of the women entrepreneurs as well as the women artisans involved.

(2) To study the problems associated with women entrepreneurship in *Japi* craft tradition.

Methodology

The research has been carried out in a village named Tilana of Nalbari district, which is one of the major *Japi* making centers of Assam. The selection of the sample has taken primarily through purposive sampling. As in the selected village named Tilana, very few people have engaged in entrepreneurial activities especially women are very less. Besides, the Observation method is used to have direct views on the village situation, schedules were also used in order to understand the socio-economic condition of the entrepreneurs especially women entrepreneurs. In-depth interviews, both formal and informal, were used among both men and women entrepreneurs of the village and the artisans worked under these entrepreneurs which have helped in understanding the perspective of them. Besides, secondary data was also collected from various sources like library, journals and so on for the study.

Result and Discussion

Women Entrepreneurs in the village

There are a few women entrepreneurs in the village Tilana. They are skilled in *Japi* making and run their own shops. There are a total of seven village shops. Each one is under one skilled artisan of the village. However, only 1 village shop is found which is run by a woman entrepreneur. The name of the shop is *K.B. Japi Udyog*. Along with other entrepreneurs, she also does the work of *Japi* making, buying from the artisans of the village and marketing of the products. She is a skilled artisan and also has participated in various expos and exhibitions outside the state. She gives directions to the worker artisans engaged in her shop and has good contacts and networks with various markets as well as customers.

Table 1: Entrepreneurs in the village

Categories	Number of people	Percentage
Male Entrepreneurs	6	85.71%
Female Entrepreneurs	1	14.28%
Total	7	100%

The above table shows that the total numbers of male entrepreneurs in the village are six which constitutes about 85.71%. However, only one female entrepreneur is found to form only 14.28%.

Under the one women entrepreneur in the village, there is a total of 20 artisan families who are dependent on the shop of the only women entrepreneur in the village. Along with the other entrepreneurs in the village, she also takes lead in *Japi* making activities and also takes care of the major activities like the marketing of the products, providing advance payment to the artisan households on the basis of profits so that the families under each artisan can buy the necessary raw materials and also some amount they use for buying their day to day necessities and so on. The artisans worked under the woman entrepreneur of the village mostly do the decoration work of the *Phulam Japis* such as cutting and making the letters for writing the names over the *Japis*, putting colorful metallic *Chumkis,* and many. However, the artisans worked from home mostly make the frames of the *Japis* and give those *Japis* to the shop. In the case of distribution of the profits, the woman entrepreneur shares the profits with the artisans. The details of the information are mentioned in the following table.

Table 2: Cost of *Japis* and share among artisans

Types of Japis	*Total cost of raw materials (Rs.)*	*Selling price of each Japi (Rs.)*	*Share given to artisans per Japi (Rs.)*
Halua Japi	40-50	50-60	10-15
Phulam Japi	60-70	80-150	30-40

The above table shows that the *Halua Japis* are sold to the buyers at the cost of 50-60 rupees each *Japis* approximately and the share given to the artisans each *Japi* is around 10 to 15 rupees. However, in the case of *Phulam Japis*, the cost is approximately 80 to 150 rupees and the share given to the artisan ranges from 30 to 40 rupees each *Japis*. The woman entrepreneur takes the orders from various business networks and according to the requirement she sends the *Japi* products to the destined locations all over Assam.

Table 3: Women artisans in the village

Categories	*Number of artisans*	*Percentage*
Male	86	85.14%
Female	15	14.85%
Total	101	100%

The above table clearly shows that among the sample of *Japi* making artisans, only 14.85% are female. However, 85.14% are dominated by males. This table reveals the dismal proportion of women artisans in the study village.

The socio-economic condition of the women entrepreneurs and the women artisans

Table 4: Age structure of the women artisans

Age Group	*Percentage of the Women Artisans*
25-35	28.57%
35-45	57.85%
45-55	14.28%

Table 4 shows that the woman entrepreneur and the women artisans in the village are of middle age. Among them, 28.57% are included in the age group of 25 to35 %. Whereas the age group of 35-45 constitutes about 57.85% of the total women artisans in the village. Only 14.28% are included under the age group of 45-55.

Table 5: Educational status of the entrepreneurs

Educational Status	*Percentage of the women Artisans and Entrepreneurs*
Under Matric	61.42%
HSLC Passed	27.30%
HS Passed	11.28%
Graduate	Nil

The women artisans and entrepreneurs in the village are not highly educated. Only 11.28% have passed higher- secondary examination however, 27.30% have passed HSLC examination and 61.42% represented by under matric category. There are no graduates among the women artisans and entrepreneurs.

Table 6: Income of the woman entrepreneur and women artisan

Income Pattern	*Percentage of the Wome Artisans and Entrepreneurs*
3000-6000	83.71%
6000-12000	14.28%
Above 12000	2.01%

The above table shows that 83.71% are included under the category of 3000-6000. However, 14.28% are under the income group of 6000-12000. Only 2.01% are included under the category above 12000.

In the study village, the main source of funds is from the family. However, very few are dependent on funds on their close relatives, friends, money lenders, and some other personal sources. The women artisans and entrepreneurs are very much disappointed with the administration as in spite of urging the government and giving many applications, the administrative machinery has not given proper attention towards the artisans of *Japi* craft. Hence, the women entrepreneurs along with men entrepreneurs need to arrange their funds on their own to continue this occupation.

Challenges faced by the women artisans and entrepreneurs

Women often become the victim of various societal barriers. They have to face a lot of obstacles while growing in any field. Simultaneously, the women engaged in *Japi* making activity also face various problems.

The family obligation is a major constraint in the development of women entrepreneurship in *Japi* making activity. Traditionally women are responsible for the household works. It is also applicable in *Japi* making society of Tilana village. Therefore, women are not able to dedicate enough time to *Japi* making. As *Japi* making activity is a labor-intensive activity, the family members and the male owners of the village craft shops do not believe in their capability to run both household work and *Japi* making activity together.

The women of *Tilana* village also face the problem of health issues. Health is important for conducting any work. Women are often restrained from working due to various health issues such as pregnancy, menstruation-related diseases, and other health problems. Besides, during the menstruation period, women are not allowed to do *Japi* making. Hence, these factors together create the problem and eventually affect the entire *Japi* making activity.

Moreover, the lack of self-confidence is another challenge for women. Mostly in rural areas, women are not encouraged to get themselves involved in earring activities. The people involved in *Japi* making activity have no faith in women and hence they are reluctant to provide entrepreneurial opportunities among women.

Lack of education also contributes towards the dismal growth of women entrepreneurship in *Japi* making society of Tilana village. The majority of the female population of the village are not highly educated and also lack innovative ideas. Therefore, they are not encouraged to engage in *Japi* making activity. Besides, financial institutions are also not in favor of giving them financial aids for the development of entrepreneurial activities. These challenges are being faced by the women of the *Japi* making society of Tilana village. Thus, in spite of having a lot of potential the entrepreneurial activities are still untapped.

Conclusion

Japi making activity forms an important traditional craft industry of Assam. It has a huge potential of contributing to the economic development of the local area along with the entire state. In this regard, women can also contribute towards the development of *Japi* making activity. However, women are not motivated to take initiative for the betterment of the *Japi* craft. Women of the village often face various hurdles. The few women entrepreneurs and women artisans who have taken the risk to continue this age-old craft making tradition are also facing a lot of troubles mainly due to financial crunch, social factors, health issues and so on. Some of the recommendations for the improvement of entrepreneurial opportunities among women in *Japi* making activities are creation of awareness programs among the people of the village to encourage women entrepreneurship, vocational training courses for the development of their traditional skills, financial assistance to self-help groups for women entrepreneurs in order to create capital funds and to mobilize resources, etc. Besides, the arrangement of some exposure trips for the women artisans along with the male artisans, improvement and easy access to health facilities, etc. is of great need. Hence, if the women of the village Tilana will be equipped with proper guidance, skills, facilities and also be assisted with adequate financial assistance then they can definitely be engaged in the entrepreneurial activities and eventually can create plenty of employment opportunities in the village.

References

Baruah. S. K., 2012, *Assam Abhidhan*, Banalata, Guwahati.

Desai.B., 2011, *Entrepreneurship Management*, Himalaya Publishing House, Mumbai.

Goyal. M. et.al., 2011, "Women Entrepreneurship in India: problems and Prospects" in *International Journal of Multidisciplinary Research,* Vol-1, p-195-207.

Kumar. P., 2017, "Concept and Problems of Women Entrepreneurship in Micro, Small and Medium Enterprises in India" in *Journal of Applied Research*, Vol-3 (7), p-5-9.

Moore. D. et. al., 1997, *Women Entrepreneurs: Moving Beyond the Glass Ceiling"* SAGE Publications, Thousand Oaks.

Sugaraj.J.M. et.al., 2014, "A Study of Women Entrepreneurship and Their Problems in the Development in Western Maharastra" in *IOSR Journal of economics and Finance,* Vol-3. P-79-83.

https://industriescom.assam.gov.in accessed on 28/04/2018.

Chapter - 10

A Study of Ethnomedicinal Plants used by Khamti Tribe of Narayanpur Block, Lakhimpur District

Nitusnata Saikia

The North Eastern state of Assam is rich in plant biodiversity as well as in ethnic diversity and has great traditional knowledge based on plant resources. In this age of modernization various tribal communities of North-East India more or less dependent on medicinal plant components for the treatment of diseases. Medicinal plants are those plants that are commonly used in treating and preventing specific ailments and diseases. The main objectives of the study were about the Khamti tribes of Lakhimpur district and their traditional knowledge of herbal plants. They have their Society, culture and traditions which are unknown treasures for the Anthropologies, Botanists, Sociologists and the Researchers. In tribal communities, medicinal plants play an integral source of easily available remedies within healthcare systems. All the plant species were collected through personal interviews, questionnaires, observation and personal interaction with medicine man (kobiraj) herbal practitioner, chauman (village head) and local elderly men and women. Different plant parts such as bark, bulb, leaf, fruit, stem, root, tuber and rhizome were found to be in use by the Khamti tribe as a medicine for treatment of various ailments and diseases.

The Khamti tribe is a sub group of the Shan people found mainly in Burma and Arunachal Pradesh but a small number of this community can be found in Assam also. They are known as Hkamti by the Burmese and Khampti by the Assamese. Their total population is 13100 as per the 2000 census out of which 4235 live in Burma. The name Khamti means ‘a land full of gold’ (kham means ‘gold’ and ti means ‘place’). They can hardly be called a “hilltribe”, as they live entirely in the plains areas near Noa-Dihing and Tengapani rivers. According to the 1971 census, their total population is 4087. In 1850, a fresh batch of about 300 to 400 Khamtis migrated to Assam under a chief from Barkhamti area. They settled a few miles above the old outpost of Saikhowa, not far from the Noa Dihing.The Khamti community consisted of three main classes, the Chiefs, the priests and the slaves. The Khamti people are Buddhists and are believer of the Hinyan sect of Buddhism.

There are various classes among the Khamtis viz Luk-khun, Lung-king, Khong-yek, Khong-lung, Chaukhun, Chebhai, Khan-flu etc. Once on the socio-political angle the Khamtis were divided into two groups as – Lu-kam and Nuk-tai. The Khamtis who migrated into Assam belonged to all the seven principalities of Khamti-Long. The various sub-groups of the Khamtis are- Namsoom, Manchuj, Long-Keng, Khankew, Simit, manlong, Monpong,Moungkang, Mounglang, Mein, Singkai, Longehot, Mannow, Mannoi and Manchuy khun.

According to the World Health Organization, over 80% of the world's population or 4.3 billion people rely upon such traditional plant based systems of medicine to provide them with primary health care. Around 3000 plants species are known to have medicinal properties in India. Medicinal plants have long played important roles in the treatment of diseases all over the world (Fallah-Hoseini H, Fakhrzadeh H, Larijani B, Shikhsamani; 2006). From the immemorial time the plants are use as medicine by the various tribal communities. Medicinal plants are a source for a wide variety of natural antioxidants and are used for the treatment of diseases throughout the world (Rafieian-Kopaie M, Baradaran A. Plant's antioxid; 2013). Medicinal plants may be defined as those plants that are commonly used in treating and preventing specific ailments and diseases and that are generally considered to be harmful to humans. (Anselem, 2004). Due to rich heritage and cultural diversity, Assam is an important region for ethnobotanical studies. The culture of traditional healing of diseases using these plants is still prevalent among aboriginal tribal communities in the North-East India.The traditional wisdom of healing among tribal communities is orally transferred from one generation to the next generation through traditional healers, spiritual gurus, and elderly or sometimes ordinary.

Khamti is very rich in plant based medicinal knowledge among the tribes of Arunachal Pradesh and Assam. These plants have been the important part of the local people. Some of the wild plants have even become an important part of the culture in some indigenous people's tradition and are known to be effective against certain diseases thus getting popular and commercialized into various products.

(Prakash D, Upadhyay G, Gupta C, Pushpangadan P and Singh K K; 2012. 19 (3):1109-1116).

The aim of the present study is to analyze the use of medicinal plant used by theory ethnic community for the curing of different ailments.

The Khamptis

Khampti tribes are mainly concentrated in Lohit district of Arunachal Pradesh and the North Lakhimpur district of Assam. The Khamti, who are a part of the great Shan race, migrated to Assam only in the second half of the 18th century. This happened when Alomphra, King of Burma, caused the final dismemberment of the Shan Empire of Pong, which once touched in its extent Tipperah, Yunan and Siam, and had the city called Mongang by the Burmese and Mongmarong by the Shans themselves, as its capital. The Shans (Tai) are believed to have originally their home to the west of China. Samlonpha, brother and commander of the army of the thirteenth king of Pong, Sukempha (777 A.D) is said to have led his military expenditions as far as the Brahmaputra vally in Assam. As E.T. Dalton points out (Descriptive Ethynology of Bengal, Calcutta 1872, P. 6) , "Whatever may have been the original seat of these people, they migrated to Assam, within the last hundred years, from the country known to us as Bor-Khamti near the sources of the Irrawady, which was visited by Wilcox in 1826, and according to their own annals they had occupied that country for many centuries."

Historians say that the Khamti migrated to India from the Irrawaddy valley, Myanmar, in 1751. They settled along the Tangapani river. They later moved and now inhabit the 'lower regions drained by the Tangapani and Noa-Dihing rivers. Their territory is surrounded by dense forests of the tropical moist deciduous type.

The Khamtis are among the most civilized tribes. They have their own language which is closely related with the language of the Shans of Myanmar, China and Thailand. To speak, the Khamti tribes used a dialect of the Tai script, popularly known as Lik-Tai. The physical characteristics of the Khamti people resemble to the East Asian people.

Area of the study

An ethno botanical survey was conducted in 2016-2017 in three villages Borkhamti Gaon, Civia Khamti gaon and of Lakhimpur district. The study area of these three villages are under Narayanpur Block of Lakhimpur district. A map is prepared for showing the study areas Fig.1. The ethnobotanical information was collected through personal interviews, questionnaires, observation and personal interaction with medicine man (kobiraj) herbal practitioner, chauman(village head) and local elderly men and women of The Khamti tribes.

Collected different plant specimens were indentified with the help of standard keys of several research workers. (Ahammadullah & Nayar M P, 1986; Kumar Y, Haridasan K & Rao R R, 1980). After collection of plant species and surveys, herbariums were prepared following the standard methods (Nath V, Khatri PK.; 2010, Dahare DK, Jain A; 2010).*

Analysis

During the present ethnobotanicinal study, 53 different plant species belonging to 10 families were found to use as traditional health care services by the village of the Khamti people. Table 1 enlists the indigenous plant species commonly used by the Khamti tribe of the study area. Each medicinal plant species is provided with its scientific name followed by family, local name and their uses. The habit of using local as well as wild herbs, shrubs, climbers and trees for cooking purposes is unique to the Khamti tribe. The women are found to be more familiar with the use of the hearbal plants. It is apparent that Khamti tribe is rich in ethnomedicinal knowledge and the knowledge is being transmitted from generation to generation. Collected data were entered in to Excel spreadsheet and summarized using descriptive statistics (Höft M, Barik SK, Lykke AM; 1999).

Table 1: Ethnomedicinal plants used by the Khamti tribe of Narayanpur Block, lakhimpur district.

SL. No	*Scientific Name*	*Local Name*	*Family*	*Parts Used*	*Medicinal Uses*
1	Abroma augusta Linn.	Maimai	Sterculiaceae	Bark, Roots	Urine sensation
2	Abrus precatorius Linn.	Mikiakuiang	Fabaceae	Seeds	Vomiting, Snake bite
3	Adhatoda vasica Ness.	Bogabahog	Acanthaceae	Leaves, Bark, Root	Anemia, Gastric, Fever
4	Ageratum conyzoids Linn.	Padribha	Asteraceae	Leaves	Cut and enjury
5	Alpinia galangal Willd.	Khing Pang	Zingiberaceae	Rhizome	Skin allery caused by insect bite and microbes.
6	Andrographis paniculata Wall. ex Ness.	Hirota	Acanthaceae	Seeds, Leaves	Snake bite, Malarial fever
7	Ampelocissus barbata (Wallich)	Songra murich;	Vitaceae	Leaves	Swellings, pain
8	Asplenium nidus Linn	Yahanka	Denustaidiaceae	Leaves	Bone fracture, body ache
9	Arenaria orbiculata Royle	Lajaibori	Caryophyllaceae	Whole plant	Anemia
10	Argyreia nervosa Burm.	Motaimon	Convulvulaceae	Leaves, White fluid	General body pain
11	Asparagus racemosa Willd.	Sottish Sora	Asparagaceae	Tubers	Impotency

(Contd...)

* Please see map of Assam & map of Dhemaji District at page 131

12	Blechnum orientale Linn.	Kalasona	Blechnaceae	Leaves	Skin itch
13	Blumea balsamifera DC.	Yanang	Asteraceae	Leaves	Diabetes, Body pain
14	Bonnaya bracheata Limk	Yakio	Schropulariaceae	Leaves, Roots	Urine sensation, Tuberculosis
15	Calamus tenuis Roxburgh	Moon khum	Arecaceae	Stem, Root	fractured bone
16	Cassia hirsuta Linn.	Kungu	Ceasulpiniaceae	Bark	Chronic gastric
17	Chloranthus erectus Munch.	Yasinha	Chloranthaceae	Leaves	Elephant foot Swelling
18	Cissampelos pareira Linn.	Tonabi	Menispermaceae	Tender leaves, Stem	Unwanted pregnancy
19	Citrus limon Burm. f.	Hatta	Rutaceae	Fruit	Leg paralysis
20	Coleus forskohlii Briq.	Moyamuksii	Lamiaceae	Leaves, Stem	Knee pain
21	Croton roxburghii Bolar	Hongki	Euphorbiaceae	Root	Bone pain, Cancer
22	Croton tiglium Linn	Saklang	Euphorbiaceae	Leaves, Flowers	Malaria
23	Cyperus flabeliformis Rottboel	Yahukom	Cyperaceae	Roots	Bone fracture
24	Datura innoxia Mill.	Pukumii	Solanaceae	Leaves	Rabies
25	Eranthemum palatiferum Ness	Murmuchi patta	Acanthaceae	Leaves	Stomach pain
26	Euphorbia hirta Linn.	Dudboon	Euphorbiaceae	Leaves, Roots	Anemia
27	Euphorbia ligularia Roxb.	Sepak	Euphorbiaceae	Leaves, Stem	Difficulty in delivery
28	Ficus hispida Linn. f.	Mukonpong	Moraceae	Bark, Roots	Tuberculosis
29	Hauttuynia cordata Thunb	Punkyo	Piperaceae	Leaves	Dysentery, Indigestion
30	Ipomea aquatica Forsk	Humen	Convulvulaceae	Leaves	Asthma, Loss of appetite
31	Kaempferia galanga Linn.	Ban hom	Zingiberaceae	Rhizome	Flatulence
32	Lasia spinosa Linn.Thwaites	Siben jeng;	Araceae	Leaves	Pain
33	Leucas aspera Spreng	Dulon bon	Lamiaceae	Leaves	Sinusitis, Earache
34	Mentha piperita Linn.	Balasen	Lamiaceae	Leaves	Knee pain Cough
35	Millingtonia hortensis, Linn. f.	Meteka	Bignoniaceae	Leaves, Flowers	Chest pain, Jaundice
36	Mollugo pentaphylla Linn.	Jaluk boon	Molluginaceae	Leaves, Stem	Dehydration
37	Mosla dianthera Maxim.	Ngakai	Lamiaceae	Leaves	Allergy
38	Ocimum scantum	Tulshi	Lamiacea	Leaves, Flowers	Cold and congestion Of lungs
39	Oxalis corniculata Linn.	Yasompi	Oxalidaceae	Leaves	Headache, Indigestion, Loss of appetite
40	Pennisetum macrostachyum Throm.	Hakka	Poaceae	Leaves, Root	Urine sensation Anal worm
41	Pilea trineria Wall.	Rambodusak	Urticaceae	Leaves, Bark	Muscular strain
42	Piper mullesus Buch.-Ham	Pipli/Pan	Piperaceae	Leaves, Seeds	Malaria, Cough

(*Contd...*)

Fig 1: Map of Assam

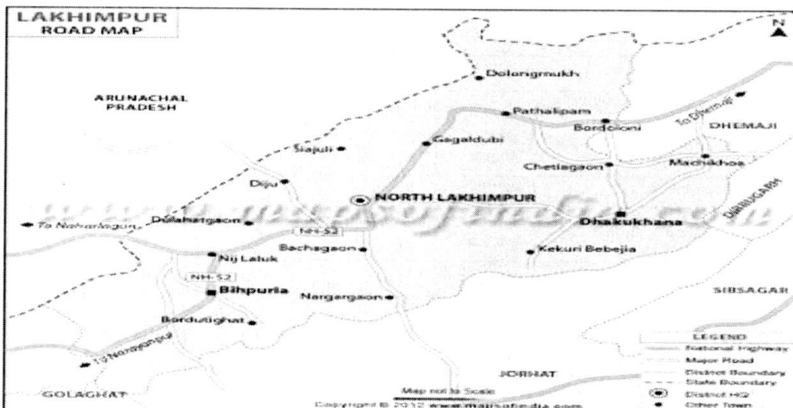

Fig 2: Map of Lakhimpur District

43	Plumbago indica Linn.	Kensumi	Plumbaginaceae	Whole plant	Bone pain
44	Solanum surattense Burm. f.	Mopu	Solanaceae	Fruits, Seeds	Rabies, Stomach pain
45	Stephania japonica Miers	Bhimraj	Menispermaceae	Tubers	Malarial feverBody pain
46	Terminalia chebula Retz.	Hellica	Combretaceae	Fruits	Cough, Chest and Stomach pain
47	Xanthium indicum Linn. Koing	chagruk	Eupharbaceace	Leaves	Muscle pain
48	Zanthoxylum acanthopodium DC.	Mekat	Rutaceae	Leaves, Bark	Stomach pain
49	Zingiber officinale Roscoe	Khing	Zingiberaceae	Rhizome	Stomach disorder, Colic and Vomiting
50	Zingiber zerumbet (Linnaeus)	Khing misrang	Zingiberaceae	Rhizome	cracks in bones

Interpretation: Present investigation documented 55 plant species used by Khamti ethnic communities of Narayanpur block under Lakhimpur district (Table. 1). This plant species included herbs, shrubs, climbers and tall trees which were collected from wild habited as well as from their home garden. The Khamti peoples are considered as one of the most knowledgeable tribe of Assam in the field of herbal medicine. The used different plant parts like bark, fruit, leaf, root, stem, rhizome for the treatment of various ailments (Table. 2). Plants used in herbal preparation are mostly collected from the wilderness in habited as well as from their home garden. This plant species included herbs, shrubs, climbers and tall trees which are use for treatment of various ailments like cough, fever, dysentery, indigestion, headache, stomach-ache, diarrhoea, skin diseases, menstrual problems and bone fracture. A majority of Khamti herbal medicine are used as paste, juice or in form of dry powder. Table 2 shows that among the different parts of the documented plants they utilise the leaves mostly (49%), followed by roots (12%), sometimes bark (8%), rhizomes/tubers (8%), stem (7%) seed (5%), flowers (4%), fruits (4%) and the whole plant (3%).

Table.2: Percentage of Medicinal Plant Parts Used

Sl.No	*Parts Used*	*Number*	*Percentage*
1	Bark	6	8
2	Leaf	34	49
3	Flower	3	4
4	Fruit	3	4
5	Rhizome/ tuber	6	8
6	Root	9	12

(Contd...)

7	Seed	4	5
8	Stem	5	7
9	Whole plant	2	3

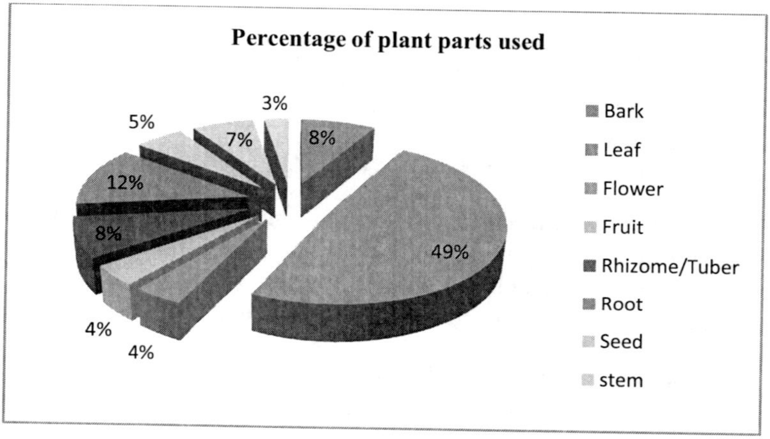

Fig. 3: Percentage of Plant Parts Used. Conclusion

The tribal peoples are mainly inhabited in remote forest area where forest resources are easily available i,e for vegetables, fruits, tubers, medicines etc. Now a days tendency towards modern treatment has increase, but still khamti people prevalent their own traditional methods to curing disease. Method and technique use by them is need to be scientifically tested for much wider practice and they keep their traditional knowledge system continue generation after generation.

Acknowledgement

The author thankfull to inhabitant of the village Borkhamti, Civia khamti village of Nrayanpur block of Lakhimpur district, whose active participation and interaction made it possible for smooth conduct of data collection.

References

Ahammadullah & Nasyar, M. P. (1986). Endemic plants of Indian region. Vol I, (Botanical Survey of India, Calcutta).

Annonymous, Report of National Seminar on Revival of Local (Tribal) Medicine sponsored by Ministry of Tribal Affairs, Government of India, Arunachal Pali Vidyapeet, Chongkham, Lohit, Arunachal Pradesh, 19th -21st November 2001.

Anonymous 2004. Statistical Hand Book of Lohit District. District Statistical Office, Lohit District, Tezu, Arunachal Pradesh.

Baradaran A, Rafieian-Kopaie M. (2013). Histopathological study of the combination of metformin and garlic juice for the attenuation of gentamicin renal toxicity in rats. J Ren Inj Prev; 2:15–21.

Bhuyan, D.K.1989. Medicinal flora of Lohit District of Arunachal Pradesh with special reference to ethnobotany. Ph.D. Thesis, Gauhati University, Guwahati.

Das, A.K. & Tag, H. 2006. Ethnomedicinal studies of the Khamti tribe of Arunachal Pradesh. Indian J. Trad. Knowl. 5(3): 317 – 322.

Prakash D, Upadhyay G, Gupta C, Pushpangadan P and Singh KK: Antioxidant and free radical scavenging activities of some promising wild edible fruits. International Food Research Journal, 2012. 19(3):1109-1116.

Jain SK, Glimpse of Indian Ethnobotany, (Oxford & IBH Publication, Calcutta), 1980, 60-94.

Pal GD, Observation on Ethnobotany of Tribals of Subansiri, Arunachal Pradesh, Bull Bot Surv India, 26 (1984) 26-37.

Haridasan K & Bhuyan LR, Medicinal Plants Distribution and Farming Potential in Arunachal Pradesh, in: BBRDT Workshop cum Training Bull, (SFRI Itanagar), 2002, 26.

Haridasan K, Sharma Anupam, Bhuyan LR and Bisht NS, Medicinal Plants Sector in Arunachal Pradesh: An overview, Indian For, 129 (2003) 37-47.

Chauhan AS, Singh KP & Singh DK, A Contribution to the Flora of Namdhapa, Arunachal Pradesh, by PK Hajra (BSI Publications, Calcutta), 1996, 161-163.

Rawat MS & Chaudhury S, Ethnobotany of Arunachal Pradesh (Nyishi and Apatani Tribes), (Bishen Singh and Mahendra Pal Singh, Dehradun), 1998, 10-14.

Hui Tag & Das AK, Plants used by the Hill Miri tribe of Arunachal Pradesh in Ethnofisheries, Indian J Traditional Knowledge, 4 (2005) 57-64.

Kant Pramode, Draft Working Scheme of Khamti-Singpho-pankhaw Anchal Forest Reserve, (Department of Environment & Forest, Government of Arunachal Pradesh Publication, Itanagar), 1998, 59-64.

Chowdhury SC, The Working Plans for the Reserve Forest of Namsai Forest Division, (Department of Environment & Frest, Government of Arunachal Pradesh Publication, Itanagar), 1994, 1-58.

Sen P.K, Working Proposal for Reserve Forest in Khamti-Singpho-Pankaw, (Department of Environment & Forest, Government of Arunachal Pradesh Publication, Itanagar), 1996, 10-72.

Dutta AC, Dictionar

Jain S K & Rao RR, A Hand Book of Field and Herbarium Methods, (Oxford and IBH Publishing Company, New Delhi), 1977.

Bentham G & Hooker JD, Flora of British India, (L Reeve & Co, 5, Henrieta Street, Convent Garden, London), 1875.

Chapter - 11

The Kingdom of the Valiant and the Scrupulous: Details of the Political Settings of the Rajputs in Delwara and Goagaon, Sirohi District, Rajasthan

Nyato Doji

When we talk about "political structure" in anthropology, we do not necessarily hint at what the lay person would understand. We speak not just of political parties contesting elections and candidates being involved in colorful dialogue. Similarly, we do not simply restrict ourselves to the tried and tested judicial system of today or the methods of maintaining order (Goldstein, 1991).

These structures today belong to a society far more complex and large than simpler societies. Simpler societies can be of the past or the present, the basic unifying feature being their smaller population size and their simpler interaction with the environment around (Goldstein, 1991).

The root of Political Anthropology can be traced back to the 19th century when Darwin's evolution had entered the social sphere; an era dominated by evolutionist where all aspects of human life, be it social or biological started to be looked at from an evolutionary perspective. Sir Henry Maine and Lewis H. Morgan where the classical evolutionist who studied the evolution of the society from primitive to an advanced form, from simple to complex societies. These classical evolutionists/anthropologists where often ethnocentric in their approach but nevertheless they laid the foundation for the growth of political anthropology. In order to understand the political organization of a particular society 'kinship study" became the focal point during that time. (Lewellen, 2003).

The area of interest of the earlier anthropologist were mostly of the simple societies but the discovery of "contextuality" in anthropological research and the shift to the study of complexsocieties led to the development of a full-fledged study of politics in anthropology. The "African political system" by "Meyer Fortes" and "Evans Pritchard" became the benchmark for the growth of the contemporary study of politics in anthropology (see Fortes & Pritchard, 1940). At present, a plethora of researches on the political life of both simple and complex societies from an anthropological perspective can be seen.

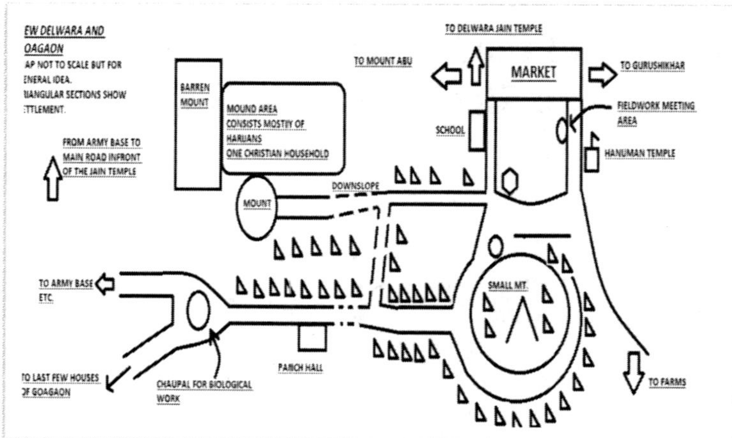

Figure 1: Hand-drawn map of Delwara and Goangaon

Universe of the Study

The present study was conducted in two villages- Delwara and Goagaon located in the Sirohi district of Rajasthan.An official Census 2011 detail of Sirohi has been released by Directorate of Census Operations in Rajasthan. According to the 2011 Census Report, Sirohi had a population of 1,036,346 of which male and female were 534,231 and 502,115 respectively. Based on the household census collected, a total of 197 households were calculated in these two villages. The majority of the village population is of the Rajputs along with a few Bhill and Brahmin population residing in these two villages. The number of members in a family averaged out from the Household census was 6-7. Mostly Hindu with rigid caste system was observed in the village and was strongly reflected in the various interviews undertaken. A strong patriarchy Dominates the Rajputs of delwara and Goagaon. Endogamy is sturdily practiced.

Methodology

An indepth interview was conducted with the villagers without any fixed sample size as the objective was qualitatively approached. The sample by and large consisted of members of various age groups and gender to get an insight and to reach the threshold for the said study. Certain key-informants were narrowed down from the lot for a detailed and an indepth understanding. Audio-visual tools were used along with both structured and semi-structured interviews. A bird's eye-view data of the various other socio-cultural spheres apart from the political structure were also studied in order to understand the political setting of the Rajputs of Delwara and Goagaon with proper insight.

Panch System

The Rajputs of the two villages have the Panch system as their first tier of political structure. The panch is an elected, formal body that consists of only men. It is extremely crucial to note that the panch is not similar to the Panchayat system.To make it amply clear, a Panchayat is a political body that is recognized by the Government of India and falls under the broader Pachayati Raj system. The Panch system is a unique political system of the Sirohi area Rajputs and though a formal body is not recognized by the Government, in that it does not formally exist on pen and paper in the Constitution.

- The panch, therefore, refers to a group of around 3-4 men (not strictly 5 like the Panchayat). They are elected by all the adult men (above 17 years or so) on grounds of "immandaari", respect, social standing, experience, seniority etc.
- The panch meet on the occasions of death, birth, marriage, settlement of disputes, festivals and for socio-economic consultation. The conflict resolution is done at three levels- familial, within the village (Internal) by consultation with the Sola Sabha and then between villages (External). External regulation depends on the severity of the issue at hand and can involve two to all sixteen villages. The panch meet as regularly as possible. Importantly, they meet for usual administrative regulation, for unusual situations such as death or dispute and on celebratory occasions such as marriages and festivals. They do not simply meet without the presence of the entire male Rajput community.
- A panch member is an adviser, a supervisor and a judge.

- The panch excludes women in all manner of decision making, execution and proceedings. The interests of women are met by the more informal meetings that women have during the evenings. Older women may also approach the panch with problems during a meeting.
- The Nagar Palika overlooks the maintenance of cleanliness, roads, street lamps etc. Everything else falls under the jurisdiction of the panch. Homicide, rape, inter-caste violence and honor killing are handled by the police. These things are very infrequent though. The panch also maintain accounts, they keep track of property divisions, and they set rules for community behavior.

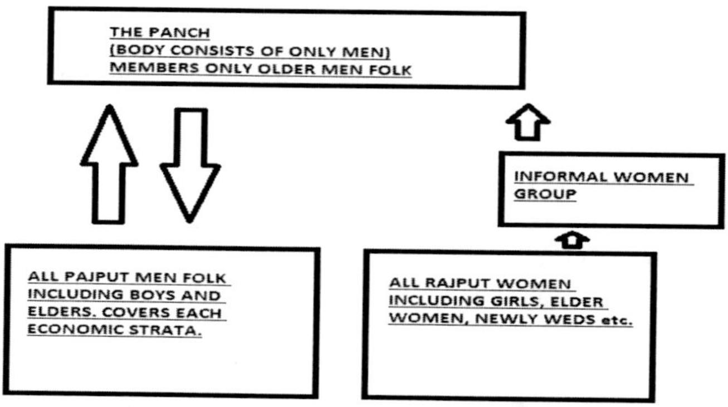

INTERNAL ORGANISATION OF THE RAJPUTS IN DELWARA AND GOAGAON.

The Sola Sabha

The sola sabha is the regulatory body of 16 villages of Sirohi district that have the panch as the building blocks. The sabha consists of the following 16 villages in geographical progression-

- Arna
- Haetamji
- Choti Dhundai
- Badi Dhundai
- Torna
- Saalgaon
- Goagaon
- Machgaon
- Saanigaon

- Delwara
- Oria
- Jawaai
- Uttroj
- Sergaon
- Kaasoli
- Esra

The sabha, like the panch, meet during birth, death, marriages, festivals and conflict dispute. Unlike the panch, the sabha gathers a lot less often. They overlook all disputes that arise between individuals or parties of more than one village. They are also the final tier of judgment of any cases that are revoked by interested parties or left unsettled at the panch level.

The sabha has its own treasury that it maintains for economic help and as a fund for times merry and dark.

The Nagar Palika

The Nagar Palika is the Municipality. The members of the Nagar Palika are elected representatives for a term of five years. The town is divided into *wards* according to its population, and representatives are elected from each ward. The members elect a *president* among themselves to preside over and conduct meetings. A chief officer, along with officers like an engineer (accountant & auditor) sanitary inspector, health officer and education officer who come from the state public service are appointed by the state government to control the administrative affairs of the Nagar Palika. The two villages get divided into 3 wards for the electoral and administrative regulation of the Palika- wards 8, 9 and 10. The 8th ward consists mostly of Bhils, the 9th mostly of Goagaon Rajputs and the Delwara areas habiting the "Harijans" and the 10th ward of the majority of Rajputs.

The Nagar Palika overlooks the sanitation of the villages. It also overlooks the construction and maintenance of roads, "boring" or tube wells. It caters to general administration and to the entire population of the two villages and not just specifically to the Rajputs. Or, The Nagar palika is responsible forwater supply, hospitals, roads, street lighting, drainage, fire brigade, market places, records of births and deaths and solid waste management.

The Police and the People

The police are involved to a minimum in the everyday affairs and conflicts of the community. They are involved only in cases of homicide, communal violence, caste violence or rape. The general consensus about the police is that they harass the public more than they assist them in problem solving.

Religious and Customary Law

In the two villages of Delwara and Goagaon, religious law and customary law are not all exclusive for the Rajputs but more of a shared feature of all Hindu castes. The customary laws are mostly caste based.For example, the Rajputs do not, by custom, eat with the lower caste groups or celebrate with them.

Very interesting tradition is one which involves the marriage of a Rajput boy with a lower caste girl. In a case study as reported, a Rajput boy ran off with a Harijan girl. He was given the social exclusion exercise. To be brought back and accepted into the community and family he had to undergo an unusual ritual. The panch had to partake of a meal and their left overs and saliva combined with water were used to "cleanse" the boy. Only then was he reaccepted into social circles though his wife was still considered of lower birth. Such cases lead to immediate abetment of all relations with her and disgrace to the family name. In extreme cases, such cases have led to honor killings.Thus, religious and customary law is mostly confined to marriage regulations and caste taboo.

Shokh Sabha Meeting of the Sola Sabha

The sola sabha for the 16 villages gather to mourn the death of any elderly Rajput members. During the Shokh Sabha everyone has to wear turbans/"murethas".The head is to be covered no matter what. Women are completely prohibited. Mostly elder members above 40 years of age are mostly present in any of such cases. Shoes are to be kept outside the entrance of the house. Everyone is seated in concentric circles with the eldest folk at the head of the gathering near the foot of the house. All other men are to be seated around them. Smoking of traditional pipes and beedis is a common feature during a shokhsabha. During any mourning offering of daliya, doodh and chach is a traditional custom.

Conclusions

Delwara and Goagaon are villages that are not entirely cut off from the fast paced life of the country. The people are simple minded but aware of the contrast between them and the settlements without. They do not have a Panchayat system but have a *Sola Sabha* instead. A deep set patriarchy runs the village political and social arrangement. The younger generations and some of the older members are open to including the youth and the women in social set ups but there is a long way to go. The villages are self-reliant when it comes to handling all economic, political and marital issues. In spite of a brutal and vicious world around, the villages are comparatively peaceful with few or no cases of homicide, rape and violence being recorded. The people dislike the interference of the Nagar Palika in their affairs. Child marriage, honor killings, caste hierarchy are far less prevalent than what our books would have us believe but not entirely unseen either. Several people are distrustful of the government that has thrown only too many empty promises at them. Honor, social relations and respect matter heavily in the society. Caste has not entirely been eradicated and seems to be a long way from there.

References

Fortes, M. & Pritchard E.E.E.(1940). "African Political System". London, Publications for the International Institute of African languages and Cultures by the Oxford University Press, H. Milford.

Godstein, A.(1991)."From Bandwagon to Balance-of-Power politics: Structural Constraints and Politics in China 1949-1978". Standford University Press, pp:31-33.

Lewellen, T.C.(2003). "Political Anthropology: an Introduction, third edition". Praeger Publishers, Westport Connecticut London, pp: 1-12.

Chapter - 12

Mother's role in child socialization

Promanita Bora

Socialization is the process of transmission of culture, the process whereby men learn the rules and practices of social groups. The process of socialization is conditioned by culture. Since every society has its own culture the ways of the process of socialization also differ from society to society. Further, the same culture and the same ways of socialization may have diverse effects on the development of the personality of the members of the same society, thus a culture need not necessarily produce stereotype personalities. There is scope for individuality in the process of socialization(Shankar Rao,2012) Socialization, in its narrow sense, tends to be confined to the social learning of children, to the process, whereby, they acquire the value of adult society so as to participate fully within it In any particular culture, it is through the process of socialization that the child acquires the attitudes and values of that culture and develops into an individual with culturally appropriate behavior patterns. In the beginning the human child comes into the world as a biological organism with animal needs. He is gradually moulded in society into a social being and learns social ways of acting and feeling. During the process, many of the interactions occur between the child and other members, particularly between parents and children. Not all parent- child interactions arise from the deliberate intention on the part of the parents to train the children. Some of these interactions arise of care taking, feeding, cleaning and protecting etc. Some are expressions of love or annoyance-reactions, which may not have direct impact on child's future, but they have significant influence on the growth and development of children's behavior. The process of caring of children starts not only after the birth, but begins right from the conception onward. Together mother and child in the parturitive relationship form a symbiotic reciprocating system necessary for each other's continued development (Bora, 2000). Thus mother is the first one who gets the first opportunity to train children. The intimate relationship between the mother and the child has a great impact on the shaping of child's abilities and capacities. She is the first persons to introduce the child to the culture of his group.

It is assumed that different patterns of child rearing will lead to differences of behavior and adult roles and thus the process of child socialization. Individual children may be given different cares or task of various kinds and the analysis of pattern of child socialization be made from their behavior in games and recreational activities, ritual and ceremonial life, or beliefs about supernatural. Children in large and busy cities may be taught to watch out for automobiles, while children in remote hilly regions might be taught to watch out for animals. In both the cases, the aim is to train the child for safety and survival. Thus it can be said that ecology, economy, social and political organizations are by and large are considered as the parameters for the behavior of the agent of socialization. Besides, through learning stories, folk tales etc. they learn many things about their culture where the family members, specially the mother play the most important role.

The Mishings

The Mishings on whom this study was conducted, is one of the significant schedule tribe community of Assam .They originally a hill tribe within the ranges of the Abor, Miri and Mishimi hills of the erstwhile North –East Frontrier Agency, now Arunachal Pradesh and they came down to the plains before the reign of the Ahom kings and since then began settling in the riverine areas of the Brahmaputra and Subansiri rivers of Assam.(Bordoloi,1987).Racially they belongs to Mongoloid race and Linguistically they are Tibeto-Burmese group. They are animistic in their religious outlook. They believe Sedi-Mc:Lo (the sky and the earth), but towards the 17th century the Mishing people came under the influence of Hinduism.

The field data have been collected from the Pani-Miri gaon in Dibrugarh district, Assam in the year 2015-2016. The village which is located about20 k.m away from the Dibrugarh town in the western direction. The village is exclusively inhabited by the Mishing people. The nearest police station of the village is Borboruah police station. The nearest bus stop is at Sessa Tin Ali which bis on the National Highway 37. The village is divided into two halves by the embankment, which is also used as main village road. The houses are constructed on both side of the road, although haphazardly.

Majority of them are of pile houses. Katcha house with thatch and tinned roof are also available. Every house of the village has atleast one loom, where traditional dresses are woven by their womenfolk. There is one Lower primary (L.P.) one Middle English (M.E) school and one high school in the village. For higher education they have to come out to Dibrugarh town.

There are about 50 families in the village with the total population of 249 including 131(52.61%) male and118 (47.38%) female. Among the 118 females 88 are found as housewives. In the present study, standard Anthropological method and techniques independently or in combination have been used in order to get the desired result.

Mother and her role in socialization

Mother plays an important role in the socialization of the children. The child first learns to relate himself to society through his mother. Next through his parents, siblings and others and later through his peers and other significant adults. Within the family the mother plays very important role in the growth of a child also. She trains the child in social values, norms and customs and to a certain extent the tradition of the family and society. It has been mentioned, "All the socialization techniques employed by the adults are probably, less effective in the modification of the child's behavior than the observation and imitation through which the children gradually absorb the skills, customs and values of their group."(Minturn and Hitchocock, 1963:331).Each family in every culture has a set of expectations and relationship which influences the eventual development of social skills, behavior and attitudes. Slowly in the process of upbringing, the child experiences different customs, rituals, beliefs, prejudices and acquires its folkways and mores. Most of the training in early childhood is not the conscious training. The unconscious training and learning with the influence of mother makes him understand to his own culture. For normal development of the infant and child social contact is necessary which is possible only within the family. When children are isolated and brought up with minimum social contact, particularly up to six years, they will show few human responses, like the 'wolf children". Therefore, for the preservation and continuity of culture, socialization is considered as the ideal way of preserving one's own culture which is first develop within a family (Barua,1998). And within a family first it is through the mother. Thus, mother plays an important role in introducing children to their society's culture.

The study reveals that the Mishing women are very hard working and polite. Except ploughing, they take active part in all the domestic works

.According to them, one of the aim of the marriage is to get a child. Motherhood improves a woman's position and a barren woman is looked down by their society. As the mother is solely responsible for upbringing of children in early stage, so it is the mother of child who plays the vital role in socialization process. When a child is born in any family, it is considered as a happy occasion. Normally a male child gets extra preference then that of a female child. The main reason behind getting preference for a male child is due to the patrilineal system of descent. Besides, there is valid economic reason behind it when a child is born; at least a period of one week or till the falling of a naval cord is regarded as polluting period. There is no restriction before and after birth for any kind of work. There were a few recorded cases, where women were found to do all types of domestic work even before the day of child birth. Birth of a baby indicates a new phase and the child is formally welcomed to the family by observing various rites and rituals. The purificatory ceremony in connection with birth is referred as Hushi. They perform the purificatory rite, soon after the remnant of the umbilical cord has dried and dropped off. Generally this ritual is performed either on the chang or on the courtyard in front of the platform. On that day a tuft of hair of the newly born is cut down by ther father himself and the removed hairs are then mixed with cow dung and is pasted on the wall of their pile house. Then purificatory water santipani is collected from the village hatula (religious personality) which is prepared after mixing milk ,cowdung, duboriban, a little amount of rice and flowers. This encxhanted water is then sprinkled on the mother and the baby and throughout the chang (pile house) with dog's tooth grasses. It is believed that enchanted water will purify the mother along with her baby and the whole Akum. After sprinkling Santipani an Astrologer or a fortune teller is approached who normally select the name of the child. The child automatically gets the surname of his/her father and becomes a member of the father's clan. The invited guest then blesses the child and mother and from that day, the child is socially accepted by the community. The first child socialization process in every Mishing's family and culture starts after passing these rituals where mother and other family members take every responsibility.

Mother as caretaker

After giving birth to a child, a mother takes every possible care according to their living condition to give a good foundation to her children. Normally, mother is the primary care taker of her children .At the same time, she seek the help of her mother-in-law, husbands sister, who are termed as secondary care taker. The role of secondary care taker is equally important, who look after the children, when the mother is out of the house, during harvesting, plantation and other works. Various studies indicate that the types of family play a role in forming different characteristics. Children in large families are severely disciplined and infant indulgence is likely to be high in joint families (Whiting 1961).Bisht and Sinha (1981:51) reported that the child in a joint family is guided in his behavior and attitude by external sources; such as grand-parents, parents and other relatives, while the child in a nuclear family is encouraged to develop his inner capabilities and interests, thereby resulting in a variegated and more differentiated self. Among the Mishings the children are given instructions verbally at home by their mother. Besides verbal instructions, they get scope for observing and imitating the elders work. An attempt has been made to find out how Mishings mothers rear their children in early stage.

Table - 1: Care Taker in Infancy

No. of women	Solely by mothers	Mother + Secondary care taker	
88	63	25	

From the table-1, it is revealed that there are 63 cases, where mother was the only care taker in early stage .In such cases; they had to take the children while going for harvesting and sometime for plantation also. Whereas, there are 25mothers who reported that they took the help of secondary care takers and in most cases they were either mother-in-low or husbands sister. They were getting the help from kin members, because in rural areas, kin members are always ready to offer help at the time of crisis.

Parents influence the children by their action, what they do on a given occasion. Anything a parent does to a child or with a child has its aim to control the child, to change or to maintain particular form of behaviors and this influence the child's action (Barua and Bharali,2000) .Sometime, parents deliberately try to change the children. As Sear's, Moccoby and Levin (1957,quoted from Kuppuswamy 1974:47) writes.' Actually every interaction between two people has an effect both on their present actions and on their potentialities for future action. An affectionate hug not only influence what the child is doing at the present moment ,but adds a small change into his expectation of what will happen in future on occasion .This expectancy in turn increases decreases the probability that he will act the same way in future. The process of influencing the child is greatly facilitated when the child develops his language skill. The words 'good' and 'bad' become very powerful to modify the child. These can become much more effective than either emotional expression or actions like beating etc.to enable him to learn the appropriate ways of behaving in the given situations. Learning and understanding culture is simple in primitive society. "Most of what a child learns in primitive society is acquired in a context of real as opposed to artificial training situations; that is to say, it does not occur in situations specially designed for educational purposes. A child learns in or near the village, in the fields or by accompanying adults on hunting or fishing expeditions. These are carried out a places and at times determined by the needs of the community, their geographical environment, and their specific types of economy"(Piddington, 1963:180). The Mishing community still retain many of the characteristics of simple society and the children are outside the influence of complex atmosphere. A child can learn more easily by imitation but in most society, obedience is expected from the children.

An emphasis has been made to find out the expectation of Mishings mothers regarding obedience from children and types of punishment they think suitable for correcting the children. Some parents expect their children to obey immediately-others leave it to the child to do things when they wish. The Mishings children are hardworking and obedient, but at the peak stage of their carrier, the children are to remain busy in their household duties. The children are brought up in usual, natural setting .The parents are not much concerned about their upbringing .As most parents are illiterate, they naturally cannot project a definite goal before their children. While interviewing the mothers, regarding the mode of obedience from the children, it is found that they are not sure about the answers. The following table reveals about the type of obedience preferred by the respondents.

Table - 2: Type of Obedience

Total No. of Mothers	*Type of Obedience Preferred*	*Total Nos.*
88	Immediate	58
	Others	30

From the table 2, it is clearly found that there are only 58 mothers who emphasized about immediate obedience from their children. They are in opinion that the children should obey their elders. While there are 30 mothers who casually remarked that they do not give much stress on it. It depends on the nature and urgency of the request and the belief that the child will know enough to do it when he can reasonably manage it. To have an idea about the type of punishments they think appropriate, for their children mothers' views were taken into consideration.

Table - 3: Punishment for Slight Offence

Total No. of Mothers	*Type of Punishment*	*Total Nos.*
88	Physical	32
	Others	56

The table - 3 reveals that the village mothers normally do not go far physical punishment. Only in exceptional cases, they go for it and that too depends on age. From the observation and interview, it is revealed that they are not much serious about the punishment and children are comparatively free and as reported do the job whenever they wish. The physical punishment is rarely imposed, whereas other type is imposed frequently. Other punishments indicate mainly scolding, isolation etc.

In primary education, generally no punishment for incompetence or backwardness, success or failure providing the necessary sanction. But discipline in matter of social custom form part of many primitive educational systems. "Thus in Samoa, we find that adults allow a considerable amount of latitude to children, while in other communities, such as the Chaga ,correct behavior is enforced by strict discipline, including form of physical punishment.''(Piddington, 1963:181).However in most cases "Simple people would agree with Bernard Shaw's saying that a child should never be punished except in anger."(Piddington 1963:182).

The concept of obedience and punishment no doubt varies from culture to culture but intra-cultural variation is also noticed due to education. On the basis of education, slight variation is noticed among the Mishings also. The mother's role regarding the child socialization varies due to economic condition, types of family structure, literary position of the parents etc.

The children in between 5 to 6 years used to go to school .There are also few incidents, where the children were deprived from school education. In most cases, economic condition is the main reason behind not getting proper education .Moreover, when a child attains the age of 10/12 years, he/she has to perform some household duties like ploughing, marketing, harvesting, repairing of houses in case of males and washing of clothes and utensils, plantation and harvesting in case of females .The children also do not mind to perform the domestic works .So they do not get sufficient time for their studies. The parents hardly contribute for their children's study mainly because of illiteracy .When enquired whether they were taught before going to school, in most cases the reply was negative. Though the children are not given formal education before 5 years, yet it is noticed that mothers all the time give training, like how to behave towards the elders or junior members of the family. Throughout the year, the villagers of the Pani-miri gaon observe different religious-cum-festivals which are performed in their family as well as community level. These festivals the children from their infancy accompany their mothers, for which their children learns the customs and tradition of their society by simply observing each and every activities. In this way they are socialized. But this role and activities of the mother and children also change along with the developmental phase.

Conclusion

A study on the role of mother towards child socialization among the Mishings mothers of Pani–Miri gaon of Dibrugarh district, Assam revealed that their children are socialized normally as per their custom and traditions. Not much formal tanning is given to their children for socialization. The children are brought up in a usual and natural setting . The parents are not much concerned about their upbringing. The first child socialization process among the Mishing's family of Pani miri gaon starts after passing the rituals hushi where mother and other family members take every responsibility. Their children are given instructions verbally at home by their mother. Besides verbal instructions, they get scope for observing and imitating the elders work. Though the children are not given formal education before 5 years, yet it is noticed that mothers all the time give training, like how to behave towards the elders or junior members of the family. Besides, through learning stories, folk tales etc. they learn many things about their culture where the family members, specially the mother play the most important role. This way the mother plays an important role in the socialization of the children.

References

Barua, I. 1998. Family and socialization processes: A study among the Tai Buddhist Communities of Assam, in North East India Ethno Cultural Perspectives and Process, edited by AK Danda, BK Das Gupta, A Basu and J Sarkar, Indian Anthropological Society, Calcutta.

Barua, I and A.Bharali.2000. "Mothers view towards child socialization:A case study among the Deoris of Assam" in Bulletin of The Deptt. of Anthropology. Vol.28, pp. 31-41: Dibrugarh University.

Bisht. S and D. Sinha.1982. "Socialization, family and psychological differentiation". In Socialization of the Indian Child, ed.by D. Sinha. Concept Publishing Company, New. Delhi.

Bora, P. 2001 Child care and development: A case study among the Misings of Dibrugarh, Assam(An un-published Ph.D Thesis of Dibrugarh University).

Bordoloi, M.N.1987. Tribes of Assam (part-I),Guwahati: Tribal research Institute.

Kuppuswamy. 1974. Child behavior and Development. N. Delhi, Vikash publishing house Pvt.Ltd.

Minturn L and J.T Hitchcock, 1963. "The Rajputs of Kolapur India" in Six Cultures, Ed. B.B Whiting N.York: John wiley and Sons.

Piddington. R, 1963. An introduction to social Anthropology. Vol. II. London: Oliver and Boyd Ltd.

S. Rao, C. N, 2012. "Socialization and Culture" in Sociology: Principles Of Sociology with an introduction to Social Thought. New Delhi: S.Chand & Company Ltd.

Whiting, 1963 Six Cultures: Studies of Child Rearing, New York: John wiley and Sons.

Chapter - 13

The Ethnomedicinal practices among the Mishings Tribe of Lakhimpur District, Assam

Purabi Gogoi

India has been known to be a rich repository of medicinal plants. Plant extracts have been used in traditional medicine for several thousand years and some plants contain certain phytochemicals that have effects on the body. Ethno-medicine is concerned with the study of medical system from the native point of view. The ethno-medicinal approach proves particularly useful for the study of indigenous therapeutic agents because it allows understanding and treatment pattern according to native explanatory models instead of only through the lens of biomedicine. Ethno-medicine is sometime used as synonym for traditional medicine. Study of traditional medicine practices which concern with cultural interpretation of health, disease, illness and also address healthcare. Ethno-medicine has been recognised as an important field of anthropology now a day. It has been defined as 'those beliefs and practices relating to diseases which are not explicitly derived from the conceptual framework of modern medicine (Pool and Geissler, 2005; Chakravorty et al., 2013; Malik et al., 2015).

Wold Health Organisation (WHO) estimated that now a day as many as 80.0% Of the world population depends on traditional medicine for their primary health care needs (Azaizeh et al. 2003). The beginning of the medicinal uses of animal in human history are well define animal and their product were part of the primary resources that ancient and modern uses could be as food or for treating their illnesses (Upadhya et al., 2014; Deb et al., 2015; Vijayakumar et al., 2015).

Documentation of traditional knowledge on ethno-medicinal use of plants has been considered as a high priority among indigenous or tribal populations. Studies were already conducted to document the practices and use of innumerable number of plant and animal species were used as ethno-medicine among the tribal and non-tribal populations of India and Northeast (Singh et al., 1996; Joseph and Kharkonger, 1997; Medhi, 1995; Hajra et al., 1997; Dutta et al., 2000; Kohi, 2001; Badola and Aitken, 2003; Saikia and Hussaian, 2004; Barua et al., 2007; Shankar et al., 2012; Teronpi et al., 2012; Chakravorty et al., 2013; Pan et al., 2013; Deb et al., 2014; Upadhya et al., 2014; Chander et al., 2015; Malik et al., 2015; Vijayakumar et al., 2015). Tribal people often depend on herbal medicines and the traditional knowledge practitioners have rich knowledge about the ethno-medicine use and practice serves as their healthcare service providers. It is evident that the traditional knowledge of the ethno-medicinal practices is generally handed down orally through generations. These plants attained a significant role under the healthcare and disease treatment and prevention of the tribal populations residing in Northeast India. Efforts to ensure their documentation are imperative in order to prevent its loss, either because of natural calamities or lack of interest among younger generations in carrying out their tradition. Therefore, such exploratory researches on ethno-medicinal use and practices of plants are not sufficiently conducted especially targeting the remotely located indigenous and tribal populations residing in rural areas in the North-east India. Therefore, the objectives of the present study are to document the ethno-medicinal practices among the Mishing tribal population of Assam.

The Subjects; Mishing Tribe

The Mishings are erstwhile a hill tribe of Arunachal Pradesh and has become second most populated scheduled tribe (plains) of Assam. Ethnically, they are Mongoloid and belong to the Indo-Tibetan linguistic group. Mishings were hunting, fishing and gathering tribe, and as a plains tribe in Assam besides cultivation, they also resort to fishing; however, hunting is rare. They construct their houses in raised platforms about feet above the ground. A typical Mishing house is sometimes as much as 30/40 m in length and contains 30/40 persons living in a hall without compartments. The pigs and looms are kept under the platform of the house. The fireplace called *meram* is considered as an auspicious place. Rice beer or apong is regarded as a popular and prestigious drink in their socio-religious life. The morung or the bachelors' dormitory is an important institution. Every village has a kebang, which can aptly be compared with a village panchayat, which acts as the governing body. The Mishings originally believed in animism; however, the present religion is the synthesis of animism and Hinduism. In spite of diffusion, they worship the sun (*donyi*) and the moon (*polo*). They believe in different supernatural beings haunting the earth, usually unseen. The Mishings practice clan exogamy and tribal endogamy in matrimonial system.

Analysis

From the present study it is noticed that now a days great advancement of allopathic medicine, herbal practice still plays an important role in curing various ailments in remote and rural areas of Assam. The traditional society people believe that illness might causes due to evil spirit , breach of taboo, black magic, sorcery etc.The present study provides comprehensive information about the eroding indigenous and traditional knowledge of medicinal plants used by Mishing tribal population of Assam, Northeast India. The identification of the active ingredients of the plants used by the local people may provide some useful leads for the development of new drugs and such new approaches of traditional knowledge regarding medicinal plants and laboratory analysis might help pharmaceutical industry in new chapters for the wellbeing of mankind. During the present study there are various types of plant herbs and animal product were found to use as traditional health care services among the Mishing people of the village Moinapara Dhemaji district. They are very rich in ethno medicinal knowledge. Traditionally the rural women prefer plant medicines rather than modern medicine for their personal ailments due to lack of modern facilities in the regions. In most remote areas, medicinal herbs are the main ingredients of local medicines and considered the main lifeline and frequently first choice. The highest use of herbs gives an indication of the presence of great abundance of herb species as noticed during field visits that areas very close to houses were well covered with herbs and centuries old traditional knowledge of the healers. Though the people of the study access to the health care services, yet they prefer traditional medicines for certain ailment as immediate and effective measure. The concept of health and disease are basically biological but it has a close relation with socio – cultural system of a society. The people of traditional society believe that illness might cause due to evil spirit, breach of taboo, black magic, sorcery etc. Explanation of illness and its preventive and curative measure reflect the knowledge, cultural value and tradition of the Population (Medhi 1995; Chakravorty et al., 2013).

According to Moinapara villagers the good health does not means the possession of beautiful body and health. They belief that carrying out of the normal days routine is sign of being healthy and if a person is unable to carry out normal routine then the person may be considered as ill and unhealthy. The highest tree species utilization might be associated with their potential to survive even during long dry and wet seasons; thus their abundance and availability throughout the year is higher in arid and semiarid areas. Medicinal plants growth form might be associated with different socio-cultural beliefs, ecological status, and variation in practices of traditional healers of different regions. The individuals suing the medicinal plans might be due to the fact that high number of herbs and trees in the studied regions and the higher plant utilization for physical ailments might be due to natural phenomenon associated with variety of complications. Traditional healers mostly prefer leaves and plant for the formulation of the diseases in most cases. Present findings are in line with other studies showing as the most frequently used plant parts for the preparation of different ethno medicine.

Prevalence of disease and ethno-medicinal treatment

For the treatment of different disease the villagers of Moinapara village go to the herbal medicine man of the village for their treatment, but a few elderly individuals in the community also dealing with the healing practices using the traditional knowledge of herbal medicine. The prevalence of common diseases and ethno-medicinal treatment among the tribal Mishing population in the study area are discussed below.

Table 1: Diagnosis and therapeutic used of ethno-medicine among Mishing

Name of the disease	*Diagnoses of the disease by the villagers*	*Therapeutic use /content of medicine*
Cold and cough	Coughing, sneezing, stuffy nose, body temperature and headache.	The prepare a juice leaf of tarua kadam mixed with little sugar taken for a week to get relief from cold ad cough. A mixer of honey and sweet basil with little amount of honey to be taken twice a day until cure.
Gastric	Extreme pain lower abdomen, constipation, vomiting etc	A glass of milk mixed with turmeric should be taken in empty stomach for two weeks.
High Blood Pressure	Headache, weakness	One handful fresh tender leaves of Neffafu are grinded properly with thick amount of water should be taken empty stomach early the morning twice in a week. A total of 4-5 cloves of Nohoru is taken regularly with meal.
Dysentry	Loose motion and in sever case watery stools containing visible red blood	Guava (madhuri) leafs grinded and make a paste which should be taken twice a day. Saru tengeshi of whole plant is taken with meal, once per day for 2/3 days until cure.
Tonsilliitis	Throat pain	Leta guti (Bonduct nut) grinded properly and mixed with a cup of water and gurgle twice a day until cure.

(Contd...)

Skin Disease	Pimple , acne or skin rashes	Fresh leafs of Neem tree should be boiled in water to be used for 7 days.
Headache	Extreme pain in forehead	A salt mixed paste made from the leaves of kanibish is applied on the forehead for 45 minutes.
Kidney stone	Extreme pain in lower abdomen	Dupor tenga leafs should be taken with water twice a day.
Jaundice	Yellowish pigmentation of the skin	Juice of sugarcane is good medicine for curing jaundice.
Menstruation problem	Unbearable stomach pain during period of menstruation	A glass of water Haru manimuni should be taken for 3 days empty stomach.

Table 2: Medicinal plants used by the Mishing tribe

Local Name	*Common Name*	*Scientific Name*	*Ailment*
Ada	Ginger	Zinziber officinale	Could and Cough
Tulasi	Sweet basil	Ocymum santum	Cold and cough
Leta guti	Bonduct nut	Caesalpinaceae	Tonsillitis
Haladhi	Turmeric	Curcuma Longa	Gastric
Jaluk	Black paper	Piper nigram	Feaver
Bhim kal	Banana	Musaceae	Stomach problem and dysentery
Gol Nemu	Lime	Citrus aurantifolia	Fever, Dysentery
Noharu	Garlic	Allium sativum	High Blood Pressure
Dupar Tenga	Air plant	Bryophyllum pinnatum	Kidney stone
Kuhiyar	Sugarcane	Saccharum officiarum	Jaundice
Tarua kadam	Sweet acacia Cassie flower	Acacia farnesiana	Cold and cough
Kanibish	Croton	Croton tiglium	Headache
Saru manimuni	Lawn pennywort	Hydrocotyle rotundifolia Roxb	Dysentery

Table 3: Animal Products used by the villagers as medicine

Local Name	Scientific Name	Mode of usage
Paro (Paro)	Columba livia	General weakness.
Baduli (Baduli)	Myotush luci fugus	Curing Asthma, Night blindness
Frog	Rana aurora	Curing Asthma
Kusia (yubi)	Monopterus albus	General weakness and relieve anaemia
Mou makhi (Tangut)	Appis mellifice	Curing cold and cough and fever
Puthi mass (Ngertak)	Puntius saphore	Very effective for night blindness and malaria.

Conclusion

The present observation revealed that the Northeast region is rich in wild plant having ethno-botanical and medicinal plant. Every culture has develops its own medicinal culture. They believe in supernatural power and other psychological believe to cure many serious health problems. They also believe in mantras which supposed to bring good health. Traditionally the mantras are commonly chanted by priests. But sometimes the local traditional healers also used mantras to cure disease. The traditional mantras using s for the treatment of disease like pain in chest and other parts of the body, snakebite, bleeding of women. The use of traditional medicine is still an important component of Moinapara of Dhemaji district of Assam. The traditional medicine man of the village has an adequate knowledge of the medicinal plant which is used to cure common ailments. Few common ailments like gastric, high blood pressure, Dysentery, Cold and cough, skin disease etc. The Mishings of the Moinapara of Dhemaji district of Assam also have access of modern medical facilities provided by Government of Assam, yet they prefer the ethno medicinal plants, herbs and animal product in different types of disease or aliments for immediate and effective result.

The present study concluded that tribal individuals residing in the remote or forest areas of Northeast India have great dependency on medicinal plants for the treatment of different disease or physical ailments. Studied regions contain considerable number of medicinal plants used by the traditional healers in different herbal formulations. Plants scoring high medicinal value or used to tradition healing should be further evaluated for their photochemical and pharmacological investigation. It is also apparent that the ethno-medicinal practices is only restricted to elderly and traditional medicine man and healers while young generation is totally ignorant the use. Moreover, detailed studies on ethno-medicine plants should be carried out before the extinction of this valuable knowledge among the tribal populations of Northeast India.

Acknowledgement

The author gratefully acknowledged the help and co-operation of local level authorities, village headman and participant for the successful completion of the present paper.

References

Azaizeh H, Khalil S, Said O. 2003. Ethno medicine knowledge of local Arab practitioners in the Middle East region. Filterapia 74:98-108.

Badola HK, Aitken S. 2003. The Himalayas of India: A treasury of medicinal plants under siege. Biodiversity 2003, 4:3-13.

Barua U, Hore Dk, Sharma R. 2007. Wild edible plants of Majili island and Darrang District of Assam . Indian journal of Traditional Knowledge 6:191-194.

Chakravorty J, Ghosh S, Meyer-Rochow VB. 2013. Comparative survey of entomophagy and entomotherapeutic practices in six tribes of eastern Arunachal Pradesh (India). J Ethnobiol Ethnomed 9:50.

Deb L, Laishram S, Khumukcham N, Ningthoukhongjam D, Nameirakpam SS, Dey A, Moirangthem DS, Talukdar NC, Ningthoukhongjam TR. 2015. Past, present and perspectives of Manipur traditional medicine: A major health care system available for rural population in the North-East India. J Ethnopharmacol 169:387-400.

Dutta AC. 1985. Dictionary of Economic and Medicinal plants. Khelmati Jorhat, Assam.

Dutta PK, Dutta BK. Medico – ethnobotanical studies on some North East Tribes / Ethnic community settled in Barak Valley, Assam : National seminar on environmental issue and priorities :challenges of millennium , 2000, Abstract Vol; 6-7.

Engel N, Ganesh G, Patil M, Yellappa V, Pant Pai N, Vadnais C, Pai M . 2015. Barriers to Point-of-Care Testing in India: Results from Qualitative Research across Different Settings, Users and Major Diseases. PLoS One 14;10(8):e0135112.

Gogoi N. 2014. Traditional medicinal system: An appraisal', Future Prospects of Ethno Medicine. P2-14 . Dhemaji Girls college, Assam.

Hajra PK, Baishya AK. 1997. Ethnobotanical notes on the Mriris(Mishing) of Assam plains : Contribution to Indian Ethnobotany, (ed . Jain SK) Scientific Publication, Jodhpur, p161-169.

Islam M. 1996. Ethnobotany of certain underground parts of plants of North Eastern region. J Ecan Taxon Bot Add Ser 12: 338-343.

Joseph J, Kharkonger S. 1997. A preliminary ethnobotanical survey in Khasi and Jaintia Hills, Meghalaya: Contribution to Indian Ethnobotany (Ed. SK, Jain). Scientific Pubiction, Jodhpur, p-187-194.

Kohi YP. 2011. Non Traditional foods and ethnobotanical plants of lower Subansiri district of Arunachal Pradesh, Arunachal Forest News 19: 167- 171.

Malik ZA , Bhat JA , Ballabha R , Bussmann RW , Bhatt AB. 2015. Ethnomedicinal plants traditionally used in health care practices by inhabitants of Western Himalaya. J Ethnopharmacol 172:133-44.

Medhi B. 1995. Ethnomedicine: A study among the Mishings in Rural Context. Bulletin of Department of Anthropology, Guwahati University 9:61-68.

Pan S, Neeraj A, Srivastava KS, Kishore P, Danquah MK, Sarethy IP. 2013. A proposal for a quality system for herbal products. J Pharm Sci 102:4230-41.

Pegu NC. 2005. The Mishing of Brahmaputra Valley. Kulajan, Dhemaji (Assam).

Pool R, Geissler W. 2005. Medical Anthropology. England: Open University Press, p-28.

Rivers WHR. 1924. Medicine, Magic, and Religion. London: Routledge.

Saikia A, Shadeque A. 1993. Nutritional Evalution of underexploited leafy vegetable of Asaam, Indian Journals of Agricultural Science 63:409-411.

Saikia LR, Hussian R. 2004. Indigenous fruits used as folklore medicine by Ahom and Khamti communities of Sivsagar district. National Journal of Life Sciences 2:389-394.

Shankar R, Lavekar GS, Deb S, Sharma BK. 2012. Traditional healing practice and folk medicines used by Mishing community of North East India. J Ayurveda Integr Med 3:124-9.

Upadhya V, Hegde HV, Bhat S , Kholkute SD. 2014. Non-codified traditional medicine practices from Belgaum Region in Southern India: present scenario. J Ethnobiol Ethnomed 10:49.

Vijayakumar S, Morvin Yabesh JE, Prabhu S, Manikandan R , Muralidharan B. 2015. Quantitative ethnomedicinal study of plants used in the Nelliyampathy hills of Kerala, India. J Ethnopharmacol 161:238-54.

Chapter - 14

Megalith as living tradition in Arunachal Pradesh

Shyamalee Gogoi

The practices of erecting megaliths or large stone are found in many societies of the world. This process is started from the Neolithic age, and still many societies of the world, erecting megaliths as a burial stone or commemorative one. In India, megaliths are found in many parts of this region and most of them are related with the Iron Age[1]. Beside this, in north east India, the practices of erecting megaliths are still found among the Khasi people of Meghalaya and the Karbi people of Assam as a burial and co memorial stone. In many tribal societies of North East India, it is found as a living tradition. They used it as a boundary stone, religious stone, path stone, resting stone, promise stone and watch tower[2].

In Arunachal Pradesh, though the practices of erecting megaliths is not a continuing process now a days , but they scattered in many parts of this region like West Kameng, Lower Subansiri and Tirap district in east. Though the practices of erecting megaliths are not found among the tribes of Arunachal Pradesh, but they still believed them as sacred one and offering rituals to them , which may indicate their relationship with the megaliths in past.

The megaliths found in Arunachal Pradesh are basically inhabited by the four major tribes, Sherdukpen, Hrusso, Apatani and the Nokte. Sherdukpens are found inhabiting in the Rupa and Shergaon area of West Kameng district, while the Hrusso or the Aka are found in Jamiri and Buragaon area of West Kameng district, the Apatanis are living mainly in the Ziro and Hapoli areas of Lower Subansiri and the Noktes are found in the Tirap district of Arunachal Pradesh[3].

Megaliths in West Kameng District

In West Kamaeng district the field work was conducted mainly in two fields, Rupa and Jamiri. Rupa is inhabited by the Sherdukpen people, while Jamiri is inhabited of Hrusso people. In Rupa area, the fieldwork was conducted in three areas, Jigang, Shergaon and Lumbakta.

In Jigang, a monolith was found in the top of hills, which they erected as a boundary stone in between Moshaksing and Jigang village. This boundary stone is covered by white lime and it is inhabited by the Sherdukpen community. About 9 kms far away from Jigang, towards west, there are found two megalithic sites; one is located at the high way site, near Duklokho River. The local people called this megalithic site as Lungjukthung and it is protected by ASI (Archaeological Survey of India) of Arunachal Pradesh. The megalithic site is called Lungstung, located near Chhoskorongkho River, which is two kms away from Shergaon village. Both megalithic sites are situated under the Shergaon Village Council, inhabited by the Sherdukpen community[4].

It was found that, in Shergaon the Sherdukpen people have not any tradition of megalithic erection. They neither use it as a burial stone nor as a co memorial. But they have their own mythological believes with those megaliths and in every year during the Khik Chaba festival, they offering rituals to the megalithic areas by their local Buddhist monk. The myth related to the megaliths of Shergaon is that, the megaliths of Lungjukthung and Lungstung were erected by their king Asu Gyptang. The cause related behind those megaliths are that, once a Tibetan king came to occupy the Sherdukpen area along with his soldiers and set their camp on a hill top near Shergaon village. One night, King Asu Gyptang, erected stones or those megaliths from Lungjukthung to Lungstung as a demarcation stone and set wooden post in between these two sites and set fire on the wooden post, one by one. That Tibetan king thought those fire posts as Gyptang's soldiers, who came to attack them at night with his massive force and ran away with his soldiers from Shergaon.

Lumbakta is another megalithic site under Rupa area, situated 3 Kms away from old Rupa-Shergaon Road and 11000 feet above from the sea level. Here, found a big rectangular stone, in a household boundary. The local people of this village belief it as a sacred one and offering rituals with their own traditional way. Jamiri is considered as a important area for the study of megaliths in Arunachal archaeology. More than 100 megaliths are scattered here and there, through the entire village. Jamiri is mainly inhabited by the Hrusso or Aka tribe. The megaliths of Jamiri are not in well preserved by the locals and they have not any past history or knowledge about those megaliths. In front of their King's house, many megaliths are lying in a very poor condition and they don't give any attention over it. Just one and half kilometers away from Jamiri village, there is a huge megalith lying down on the road side, which was destructed by BRO (Border Road Organization). This megalith is considered as a demarcating stone by the Local people. There is a narrow road started through this megalith up to Thrizino. They used this narrow sloppy road in past to communicate with the people of Thrizino, mainly inhabited by the Akas. The condition of this road is not good and it takes two to three days to reach the plains. In middle of the village Jamiri, another 4 erecting stones are found. They called it Thrasra and considered it as a promise stone. In every year, during Khupho puja, they offered eggs, river stones, tree roots, scorpions etc to these stones by their local priest.

Another important part of Jamiri is the stone tombs, which are found in the west direction of the village. The history behind these tombs is not known by the locals. They just informed that, these are older than their King Thage Raja. Only two tombs are found in a good condition, others are partially destroyed by the locals for curiosity. They believed it as a burial place of some unknown soldiers and have some restriction to touch the tombs.

Megaliths in Lower Subanshiri District

Megaliths in Lower Subansiri are found in the Ziro valley, mainly inhabited by the Apatani tribe. There are four megaliths, and the tallest menhir is 25' tall. Beside this tallest menhir, it has three more megaliths. This megalithic site is known as Shiva linga or Siddheswara temple. Locals believe these megaliths as Hindu God Shiva and his family – Parvati, Kartika and Ganesha and worship these. The priest, belong to Hindu religion, believe that, according to Hindu mythology, the linga has been mentioned in the Shivapurana; chapter 17. In Shivapurana, the world's tallest Shiva linga will be called as lingalaya and the entire area will be known as Arunachal.

The Archaeological Survey of India (ASI) of Arunachal Pradesh, visited many time to this site for observation, but still not considered as ASI protected area. Many outsiders, pilgrims or devotees of Lord Shiva, come to visit this place from many parts of India, and worship these megaliths in the name of Lord Shiva[5].

Megaliths in Tirap District

In Tirap, there are found three megalithic sites situated in the villages-

Borduria, kheti and Pulung. The megaliths found in Tirap has the relation with the Nokte tribe, the major tribe in Tirap district who practiced head hunting before the arrival of British government in Greater Assam. The megaliths found these sites are also related to the head hunting cult of Noktes or Namsang Naga of Arunachal Pradesh. In pre British era, they raid a village for internal feuds due to various reasons. After returning from a successful raid, every man took the head/ heads of their enemy, whom they killed and share a community fest. After the fest is over they erected stone in a particular area, with the help of their local, traditional priest against the number of heads they hunted during raid and put the heads in Morung house. They considered these stones as untouchable, accept their local priest.

Around 1920, the Noktes or Namsang Naga of Tirap, gradually left this head hunting cult, because of the pressure put by the British administrative against this practices. Christianity is a reason also, which also change their mind set. The missionaries became a stronger force for change in social and cultural practices of the Noktes. Though the Noktes converted to Christianity, but simultaneously they keep their own culture and tradition. In every year, during the Chalo Loko festival, the local priest of Noktes offering rituals to the megaliths.

At Borduria, the megaliths are found on the top of the village. Around 80 megaliths are remain there and this site is protected by the Directorate of Research; Arunachal Pradesh. The locals informed that more than 30% megaliths are misplaced from there by PWD, due to road construction.

The Present scenario of megaliths in Kheti is not in a good state. More than 100 and above megaliths are found there. But these are neglected by the locals. They fully converted themselves to Baptism and left the rituals related with their head hunting cult or megaliths.

In Pulung, there is stone found in the village and the locals believed it as a sacred one. This site is well protected with bamboo fence by the locals and offering rituals to this stone with their own traditional way. The stone was erected by an Ahom king of Assam, as a symbol of peace and harmony between Ahoms and Namsang Naga (Noktes), and from that time they believed this stone as an auspicious one[6].

Analysis

It has to be seen that, in North East India, the hills of Khasi, Garo, Jayantia, Naga and Manipur have several megalithic sites and it reflects their identity and culture. Recently the megaliths found in Arunachal pay some attention by the Scholars and researchers to study about the history behind these stones. Those megaliths found from West Kameng to Tirap district of Arunachal Pradesh, indicates the culture and identity of the people of Arunachal Pradesh, flourished during the Iron Age. These megaliths of Arunachal Pradesh also clear the doubt that, this region of India was not forbidden land during prehistoric era.

The megaliths found at Shergaon; West Kameng has its own oral history. But it has not any written record or history about these stones. If we analysis the oral history of Sherdukpens, it has to come out that, their King Asu Gyptung, who erected these stone, had a relation with the Assamese people as he married an Ahom princess from Shivasagar. The Ahoms were come to Assam through Patkai at 12th century. So, the history related to these megaliths is in between 13th to 18th century.

There is not any similarity found between the megaliths of Shergaon and Jamiri. The Jamiri megaliths are totally separated from Shergaon. The local people of Jamiri have not any knowledge about these. But they informed that these are older than their king Thaga Raja, who settled there at the time of the reign of Ahoms. From this conception, we may come to the point that, the Jamiri megaliths were may be erected before the arrival of Ahoms or in between the period of Ahom dynasty. If we notice on the structure of the Tomb, it is found that, no other tombs are found in entire Arunacahal Pradesh, and therefore it indicate a society exist there before the Hrusso or Aka tribe.

The megaliths of Ziro are isolated. These are based on the Hindu mythological beliefs as Shiva Linga or Lord Shiva and his family. Any historical or archeological work still not done on these and therefore the actual history related to these megaliths cannot be found out. Though Megaliths of Noktes has not any written history, but they have a very strong oral history about these. The British administrator also record about the culture of Noktes during the time of administration in Tirap. In 16th century, they were migrated from the border areas of Myanmar and settle in Tirap, at the time of reign of the Ahoms. Thus, it can be considered as, the process of erecting stone or megaliths among the Noktes are started during the 16th century.

The Tradition of erecting megaliths was continued from the time of their forefathers before the arrival of British in Tirap. After the arrival of Christian missionaries, they converted themselves to Baptism, and left their head hunting cult as well as the erection of megaliths, but they still offering rituals to the megaliths as a sacred one in every Chalo Loko festival

Conclussion

The megaliths found in various tribes of Arunachal not only give the information about their undated history, but also reveal the present culture, especially related to Sherdukpen, Hrusso, Apatani and Nokte. Though the continuation of erecting megaliths almost vanished from some societies, but it is still found as a living tradition in many tribal societies of North East India. The Khasi and the Karbis are still continuing the tradition of erecting megalith as a burial and co memorial stone in this region. The megaliths remain from West Kameng to Tirap district of Arunachal may prove that people of this region shared common culture in prehistoric period. Though the continuity of erecting megaliths is not found in Arunachal, but they still offering rituals to the megaliths. The purposes of offering rituals are not found same, but all are related with the religious faith on some super natural being. Therefore one can conclude that, megalithic culture is still a living tradition in interior region of Arunachal, and by observing the life of the people and their culture, we can draw an image of megalithic human civilization in Arunachal Pradesh.

References

H. C. Sharma, 'Prehistoric Archaeology of Northeast India' in TB Subba (ed) Northeast India: A Handbook of Anthropology. Orient Blacksawn, Hyderabad, 2012, p.10.

H. Bareh,'Encyclopedia of North East India' Vol 1, Mittal Publications, New Delhi, 2001, p. 1-7, 32.

M.L. Bose, 'History of Arunachal Pradesh'. Concept Publishing Company, New Delhi, 1997, p. 22-29, 35-47,54-66,96-103.

C. Sumnyan, ' British Relation with the Nocte of Arunachal Pradesh: A Study of the Namsang- Borduria Disputes' in Proceedings of North East India History Association, 35th session, 2014, p. 302-310.

Fieldwork in Lower Subansiri district of Arunachal Pradesh

Fieldwork in Tirap district of Arunachal Pradesh

Notes

1. https://www.census2011.co.in/census/district/442-sirohi.html.

Index

C

N

O

P

R

S

T

U

V